GRAND HORIZONTAL

GRAND HORIZONTAL

The Erotic Memoirs of a Passionate Lady

CORA PEARL

Edited by William Blatchford

STEIN AND DAY/*Publishers*/New York

First published in the United States of America in 1983
Copyright © 1983 by William Blatchford
All rights reserved, Stein and Day, Incorporated
Printed in the United States of America

STEIN AND DAY/ *Publishers*
Scarborough House
Briarcliff Manor, N.Y. 10510

Library of Congress Cataloging in Publication Data

Pearl, Cora, 1837-1886
   Grand horizontal.

   Originally published in English in 1890. Not to be confused with Mémoires de Cora Pearl
published in 1886 and translated into English in the same year under the title: Memoirs of
Cora Pearl.
    1. Pearl, Cora, 1837-1886.   2. Courtesans—France—Biography.   I. Blatchford,
William, 1920-   .   II. Title.
HQ194.P4   1983   306.7'42'0924   [B]   82-42870
ISBN 0-8128-2917-4

CONTENTS

INTRODUCTION

There is something of a mystery about this book.

Eliza Emma Crouch was born in Plymouth in 1837, and as 'Cora Pearl' became one of the best-known courtesans of the French Second Empire – so famous that she was even granted an entry in Sir Leslie Stephen's great *Dictionary of National Biography*. There was something of a stir when it was rumoured in the 1880s that Cora, dying of cancer in Paris, was writing her memoirs, for she had been the mistress of many prominent men – including Prince Napoléon, Prince Achille Murat, Prince William of Orange, the Duc de Morny and, it was rumoured, the Emperor himself.

When the *Mémoires de Cora Pearl* were published in the spring of 1886, however (and translated into English the same year), they proved extraordinarily dull. The pseudonyms she gave her lovers were soon deciphered (the 'Duc Citron' was obviously the Prince of Orange, 'Godefroy Dumont-Barberousse' was obviously Ludovic, Duc de Gramont-Caderousse, and 'Duc Jean-Jean' Prince Napoléon, nicknamed 'Plon-Plon'); but she said nothing very scandalous about them. It was immediately suggested that, like Harriette Wilson fifty years earlier, she had sent chapters of her autobiography to her former lovers, and had been paid to excise the racier passages. However that may be, the *Mémoires* soon sank into such deep obscurity that they were never reprinted.

The present book is another matter. It was brought to my attention eighteen months ago by a friend who had been shown it by a German collector of erotica living in Switzerland. A single volume entitled *The Memoirs of Cora*

Pearl, it was printed in English and issued in 1890 under the imprint of 'Voluptopolis'. There was, of course, no such publishing house; it was one of the many fictional imprints under which such books were issued in the late nineteenth century – others were 'Priapeville' and 'Merdianopolis'. The edition must have been very small indeed; the collector told me he had never seen another copy (though he had heard of a German edition), and I have failed to trace copies in the most prominent public collections of erotica, including the British Library, the 'Phi' collection at the Bodleian, the 'five-star' collection in the New York Public Library and the 'Delta' collection in the Library of Congress. I was, after some persuasion, allowed to transcribe the book (though in the collector's library, and without the aid of photo-copying), and am grateful for the owner's permission to publish it.

The book purports to have been written by Cora Pearl rather earlier than the *Mémoires* – perhaps round about 1873, when she was still living in the South of France with her friend, another courtesan, Caroline Letessier, then mistress of the son of the Prince of Monaco. It is certainly rather more the kind of book one might expect (or, perhaps, hope) of her, showing a great deal of spirit and a fine disregard for the feelings of any of her lovers who might read it. It is also sufficiently frank to have made conventional publication impossible, containing some of the most explicit sexual passages written by any female author until our own time.

Much erotica purporting to be written by women (including that published by the notorious 'Mary Wilson' in the eighteenth century) seems likely to have been written by men. Is it possible that the *Memoirs* are a forgery? It is almost impossible to say. There is no way of checking the intimate details of physique and erotic behaviour of Cora Pearl's lovers (though, for what it is worth, they seem to be in line with the truth where hearsay or gossip offer any evidence); and if there is nothing here which could not have been written by her, there is equally nothing which an intelligent writer who knew her and her circle could not have counterfeited. The style is very different from that of the *Mémoires*; but one would expect that, for the latter were written in French and, since Cora Pearl never succeeded in learning even to speak that language idiomatically, far less to write it, it may be true that (as has been suggested) the *Mémoires* were largely the work of the Comte Irisson d'Herrisson, a former Army officer who was a good friend of hers towards the end of her life. The present book is in idiomatic, rather careless English, somewhat 'old-fashioned', with a turn of phrase which often recalls the eighteenth rather than the nineteenth century – as one might expect of a woman brought up in a provincial town, with little experience of English as spoken in society.

It reflects much the same attitude towards life as the 1886 book. In that, for instance, she writes:

I have never deceived anybody, because I have never belonged to anybody; my independence was all my fortune, and I have known no other happiness . . .

and later

I may say I have never had a preferred lover . . . Blind passion and fatal attraction, no! Luckily for my peace of mind and happiness, I have never known either. I have always looked upon the favourite lover as a myth, or empty word . . . A handsome young and amiable man who has loyally offered me his arms, his love, and his money, has every right to think and call himself my favourite lover, my lover for an hour, my escort for a month, and my friend for ever. That is how I understand the business.

There is nothing in the present text which contradicts that. There is no doubt that money was one of Cora Pearl's great interests – though only because of what she could buy with it in the way of material goods and social position; she never hoarded money as such. As to love: the classic view of the prostitute as a woman who fundamentally hates men seems less applicable to the woman who wrote this book than to the woman who wrote, or was helped to write, the *Mémoires*. If there is anything that is obvious in these pages it is that she enjoyed physical love very much indeed; while she sold sex as a commodity, there are several occasions on which she relished it for itself alone (the episode with the boy Marcel in the gardens of the Château de Beauséjour, pp. 130 ff., for instance, and the whole relationship with André or Henri Hurion, Prince Napoléon's friend).

There are several incidents in the *Mémoires* which are omitted or slightly altered in these pages; there is evidence that the book was written very quickly, with much emphasis on the erotic passages – a sign perhaps that it was written for money. If so, presumably it failed, for there is little doubt that it was not published during Cora Pearl's lifetime. Perhaps she was saving the manuscript for 'hard times'; but when they came, during her final illness, recoiled from publishing it, and composed a less forthright substitute. Her motives may have been those which prompted Aubrey Beardsley, just before his death, to plead that all his erotic drawings should be destroyed. Perhaps passages *were* sent to some of her lovers, and they *did* pay for their suppression – there is some mystery as to where Cora got the money which kept her during her later years, when she lacked rich protectors. On the other hand it is difficult to reconcile blackmail with her on the whole rather benevolent character.

Even the reader who disapproves of the erotic element in this book will probably admit that Cora Pearl emerges rather more sympathetically from it than from her 'official' *Mémoires*; her attitude towards her lovers (of whom, incidentally, there were many more than she mentions here) is on the whole kinder, and there are traces of a much more sympathetic character than many of her biographers present – though in *The Pearl from Plymouth*[1] (1950), by far the fullest biography, W. H. Holden records that there is strong evidence that she sent money regularly to both her mother in England and her father in America, and the comments of her contemporaries, when disinterested, were also often sympathetic.

If they regarded her as a parasite, she seemed to most of them to be an engaging and amusing parasite, whose entertainment value far outweighed any harm she did. Her conduct during the Siege and during the Commune was by no means that of a selfish woman, and her good nature (if offset by an apparently fearful temper) is evident. And anyone wondering how this somewhat coarse, uneducated girl, grown into a woman far from conventionally handsome (if one is to judge by the many photographs which have survived) became the most famous courtesan of her time, might do worse than turn to the Introduction to Alfred Delvau's *Les Plaisirs de Paris*, published in 1867:

You are today, Madame, the renown, the preoccupation, the scandal and the toast of Paris. Everywhere they talk only of you: the humble to envy you, the wealthy to scorn you, the average people to adore you. As for myself, being neither poor, rich, middling nor otherwise, but being in fact impartial, I content myself by putting your name like a rose-coloured flag at the portal of this little frolicsome temple raised in honour of Parisian pleasures, of which you appear to be the most exquisite, the fullest, and the dearest personification.

William Blatchford,
Cambridge 1982

[1] Long out of print, this book, so thoroughly researched, has been invaluable in providing notes for the following text.

GRAND HORIZONTAL

CHAPTER ONE

I am born, at Plymouth – lasciviousness in the streets – school in Boulogne – a public bath – pleasures of the flesh – my shyness disappears – the seduction of Hortense – men, a source of pleasure? – the gardener's grandson – interrupted enjoyment

I was born at Plymouth, in Devonshire, in the year 1842,[1] in East Stonehouse,[2] the daughter of Mr F. N. Crouch, the noted composer whose song 'Kathleen Mavourneen' is known throughout the world, and of his wife Lydia, a lady whose singing voice was the envy of many, and whose spirited manner enabled her to bring up a large family on the uncertain income of a gentleman whose talents were never equalled by the amount of money he was able to earn through exercising them.

My early years are of little interest to the general reader: one of a number of children – I had five sisters – I grew through the years of childish play and enjoyment without incident. My parents, who had christened me Emma, were kind to me, and protected me from the rougher incursions of a world often indifferent to the nicer virtues. A great port must always be subject to periodic disturbance by the enthusiastic behaviour of men too long confined to the company of their own sex – a circumstance liable to give rise to displays of uninhibited licentiousness. A child may, however, grow up amid such scenes without necessarily

[1] actually, 1837. Cora Pearl later falsified her birth certificate to give herself five years' advantage.
[2] at 5, Devonshire Place

being affected by them, and indeed when I first came into contact with lasciviousness, I failed to recognize it.

One of my earliest recollections, for instance, was of being walked by my father through a narrow lane at the back of Union Street (the thoroughfare connecting Stonehouse with Plymouth itself, and one thus much frequented by celebrating mariners). One of the theatres[3] at which from time to time my father exercised his musicianship lay in this Union Street, and I had been allowed to sit at the back of the pit and to watch one of the later afternoon performances. Dusk had fallen by the time we left the stage door, and my father was to accompany me home[4] before returning to the theatre for the evening performance.

As we walked out into the long dark lane which led towards our home, I was conscious of a number of people lining the pavements; they were in couples, and leaned against the walls, their bodies heaving and moving one with the other, and I was conscious of a murmur of noises, of low moans and muttered expletives as we passed hurriedly by. My father took the first opportunity of turning into another street which led back to the main thoroughfare, and I was unconscious at that time of what the spectacle meant: of course it was my first display of the animal nature of sexual congress. The bodies had been those of the lowest prostitutes of the town and of willing sailors, eager to void themselves for as low a sum as possible into the nearest willing female.

Apart from this single incident, my life was innocent as a child's could be; I had no brothers to introduce me to the essential difference between the sexes. Nor was I to discover this, at first, when I found myself in a convent

[3] presumably the Palace or the Grand Theatre
[4] to 8, Caroline Place, East Stonehouse, whence the family had moved

school in Boulogne, though it was certainly there that my sexual education began. The reason for my going to France is still obscure to me, and at the time was an utter mystery. My father at first more and more frequently absented himself from home, and then vanished completely: I later learned that he had tried his luck as an actor upon the London stage, and then made for America, where he completely disappeared from our ken. My mother struggled on alone for some time, and then, being of a religious disposition and seeing the difficulties of raising a girl to pure womanhood in a naval town where loose behaviour was more common than polite usage, took advantage of the recommendation of a friend, and in 1849 put me on board a ship for the French port, where I arrived one spring morning and was escorted, by a nun dressed from head to foot in black, to the school where I was to remain for eight years.

This was situated in a large, somewhat bleak building in the Rue des Pipots, not far from the centre of the town, but so surrounded by tall walls as to be completely cut off from it. A large garden allowed us some sight of the sun, and a little exercise by tending the vegetables there; and once a week we were marched to the Church of St Nicolas, nearby. Otherwise, we were as imprisoned as any miscreants in the world.

Close confinement in a dormitory with a dozen older girls was to me from the beginning a novelty; I had formerly to be sure shared a room, and a bed, with two of my sisters; but we shared also the common indifference of young girls of the same family and sex to each others' bodies, and the degree of interest which my new companions exhibited not only in their own but in each others' bodies was something strange to me.

After I had been introduced to the Mother Superior or Headmistress of the school, I was taken by one of the younger sisters to a large room beneath the roof, where twelve beds lay side by side in a confined space. A number of girls sat or lay on their beds, engaged in mending or in reading or in idle chatter in what I took to be the French language. I was introduced to the eldest of them, Liane, who took me by the hand and led me to a bed which was stripped ready for my occupancy. My single poor sack of belongings was soon emptied into the cupboard at the bed's side, and, the sister having left, Liane took me again by the hand and led me from the room, saying something in a laughing voice to the other girls, several of whom followed. I was taken to another, smaller room on the same floor, which contained only a large tin bath and three jugs of steaming hot water which a servant had fetched.

There to my surprise Liane began to undress me; an activity which did not take long, since it being summer I wore but little. Though shy enough, for I had never appeared completely naked before anyone save my mother, I was too nervous to attempt to protect myself or to dissuade the girls who began to explore my body, passing their hands over my thin shoulders and hips and chest, where no breasts had as yet begun to bud, though I was surprised at the familiarity. I was even more surprised, however, when having placed me in the tub and poured the pleasantly hot water over me, Liane stripped herself to an equal state of nature with my own, and climbed in with me – a privilege which, I was to discover, the eldest girl in the dormitory by long custom reserved for herself. As the other girls watched, Liane took a piece of soap and thoroughly washed me, raising a lather of soap over my whole body, and paying particular attention to the little crevice between my legs, where as yet not a hair grew, but where I nevertheless experienced a sensation of warmth and a pleasant tickling new to me.

Having poured more water over me to wash away the

suds, Liane pressed the soap into my hand, and taking it in her own, passed it over her breast. I was not unwilling, however shy, to explore her body, for it was the first time I had seen that of an older girl completely unclothed. The swelling of her breasts interested me strangely, and it was with wonder that I felt the nipples raise themselves under my palms until they were as hard as little thumbs; and then, as I passed my hands between Liane's legs, I felt that between them grew an as yet sparse but soft and springy growth of hair.

It was plain to me that Liane found my washing her an agreeable process, and I concluded that she was especially eager to be clean between the legs, for it was in that region that by gesture and her own movement she encouraged me to continue to wash her, thrusting her parts into the palm of my hand. Then, quite roughly, she thrust my hand away and herself began to rub herself there with her index finger, gasping with what seemed to be especial pleasure, and with her other hand smoothing my body, passing it over my buttocks and pulling me towards her. The other girls looked on with great intensity the while, one or two of them seeming to need to adjust their *vêtements de dessous*, by the movement of their hands beneath their skirts.

After a while, Liane uttered a short, sharp word, and suddenly stopped her motions, then without a word climbed out of the tub, wiped herself briskly with the only towel that was there, and left the room, followed by the other girls. Perplexed, I dried myself as best I could, watched by a somewhat sour-looking girl a little older than myself, who seemed to have been on guard outside the door but had now entered and was watching me. Imagine my surprise when she addressed me in English.

She was, she told me, from Bristol, and had been at that school for two years.

'You enjoyed that, didn't you?' she asked me, rather bad-temperedly.

I said that I had certainly not found it unpleasant, and was at all events glad that the custom of the school seemed to be that of cleanliness – at which Bette (for that was her name) laughed shortly, and left me to find my own way back to the dormitory.

My education began that day, in more ways than one. While during the school hours I was taught French, of which I soon had a reasonable command, the domestic virtues, and the slightest glimmering of mathematics, history and so on, at night I was taught the pleasures of the body, which within a year or two became so keen that I was convinced that anyone who neglected them was a dunce indeed. These pleasures were of course exclusively female, for the sisters were careful that we should not come into contact with any male company. One or two of them were not averse to the pleasures of which I speak, however, though I never found in my years at Boulogne one who pressed lascivious attentions on any girl too young or too inexperienced to receive them with equanamity. It was a surprise to me that grown-up ladies should also find pleasure in the flesh, for I had thought for the first few months that such was a childish enjoyment only. I had not liked to discuss these matters with the older girls, and certainly would never mention them to our mistresses.

But one day at the beginning of my last eighteen months at the school, going suddenly into one of the classrooms to fetch a set of needles which I had forgotten, I discovered Bette on her knees before Soeur Rose, one of the younger and prettier of our mistresses, her head thrust beneath her skirt; and while the sister pushed her away the moment she heard the noise of my entry – for I had approached quite openly and without subterfuge – I had still glimpsed an expression on her face which was familiar to me as counterfeit of that on the faces of my friends at certain times of mutual pleasure. Later, I taxed Bette, and she told me that Soeur Rose took special pleasure from being kissed on those parts which I had not thought to be for more than one purpose; and thus was my education continued.

Our nightly experiments in the dormitory can be imagined. Eugénie, my particular friend, hearing from Bette of the incident with Soeur Rose, determined to introduce me to the pleasure the lips and tongue can give, and I did not find that pleasure at all mitigated by distaste; then as since, I was keenly conscious that one of the greatest joys in life is experiencing the pleasure that one can give to one's lovers. And now I was fully grown, and keen to experience myself the full extent of the pleasure I could give to others. For the most part, we fell into pairs, and there grew up between many of us true and real devotion, unmatched since. On other occasions, when we were especially loving, three, four or five of us would come together to see what several partnerships of pleasure could be devised, and our experiments were by no means without their effect on my later career, for I learned at that time to be wary of no activity which pleasure was the result of.

I was astonished to learn, as the result of the conversation of Eugénie and the other girls, that boys and men also felt the same keen emotion that we did, for I had thought they would be too occupied with their work to have time for such leisurely activities. I was abashed when I discovered that men expected to take those pleasures not only among themselves, but with those of the opposite sex, for this seemed unnatural to me. Part of my education in this matter was conducted by Hortense, a lively girl of fourteen, who told me that from the time she was twelve she had been the favourite of her uncle, a young farmer from Deauville who had first come to stay with her family when she was very young and had been customarily bathed in front of the kitchen fire. By inviting her brother to help to bath the young girl, Hortense's mother had unwittingly been the cause of her seduction, only a few years later – though this was conducted with as much kindness and consideration as enthusiasm by her uncle, who was only about eight or ten years older than herself, and only approached her when it was clear that she was becoming of an age when she could bear a man.

Hortense described to me her own astonishment when her uncle, taking her to bathe at a secluded pool of a nearby river one summer's day, first stripped himself naked before her, and she saw between his legs the apparatus which was soon to become her delight. Already, she told me, it was of what seemed a great size (due no doubt to the warmness of the day and her uncle's anticipation); but when she, nothing loath, stripped herself, it swelled to become (she said) like nothing so much as the handle of a trowel or some other gardening implement.

She was too curious not to wish to examine this strange tool, so unfamiliar to her, and her uncle was not so shy as to refuse her the opportunity for such an examination. Men, she told me, were possessed of this device which hung between their legs, and with which, while standing up, they performed the office we accomplished while sitting down! For the most part it was sufficiently small to be concealed without difficulty in their clothing. But when their clothes were off, it was possible for them at will to persuade this thing to swell and grow until it stood up from their body at an angle towards their bellies; and beneath it was then revealed a sort of sack in which two round objects like stones were concealed, elusive to the fingers, and also, it seemed, tender, for though when gently touched they gave pleasure, if handled roughly they gave pain and resulted in the diminution of the tool above them.

Her uncle had kindly allowed Hortense to examine the

objects of her interest closely, and to feel the strength of the tool with her fingers – it was, she said, hard as iron and gristly, though the skin could be moved over it easily enough, like the skin of a sausage not quite full, and at the top could be pulled back to reveal a knob or head, fiery red, with a small hole from which a whiteish liquid seemed to ooze. Then her uncle had examined her own body, and had been pleased, she said, to see the downy hair which grew between her legs, for at the sight of it he had grinned broadly, and told her that he was very pleased at it, and would make her a woman.

What then happened had given her some pain, for he had placed the head of his tool into the hole between her legs, and had then driven it into her with such force that, she said, she felt likely to have been broken open. The action at first she feared had broke his tool, for he gave a cry and his body collapsed upon her, and in a moment his tool, which he withdrew, grew small and soft. But he assured her that he was not hurt, not so much as she; and then he had gone to sleep on the river bank – a thing which enabled her to examine him even more closely, and to discover other differences between her body and his – such as the much greater growth of hair about him, especially on belly and thighs, and also on his buttocks which she said were furred like those of a horse or ass (something, I was later to find, not altogether the rule).

After a while, he woke, and his tool once more began to grow in size, which he helped at first by rubbing it with his hand, and then by asking her to do so, which she did with pleasure until with a grimace he pulled her hand away, saying something about not wanting to come, which she found strange, since they were not expected at home until the end of the afternoon. Then once again he placed his tool within her, but this time with greater care, placing her with her bottom upon a raised tussock of grass, and parting her legs more widely than before, so that there was scarcely any pain, and indeed as he began to move his tool in and out she began to feel a delicious and languorous pleasure, greater than any of the sensations of pleasure that she had received under the caresses of any of us in the dormitory. While she would happily encourage us to pleasure her now, she seemed persuaded utterly that men possessed the keener means of procuring her enjoyment, and looked forward to the next holidays, at which time her uncle had promised to persuade her mother to allow her to accompany him on his travelling to the south to buy cattle, and when she hoped to renew her acquaintaince with such a keen new joy.

The result of Hortense's narrative was to make me as mad to experiment with the body of a man as were the other girls to whom, with a pride that was more than a little irritating, she had told her story. But we were closely watched by the sisters, and on the weekly occasions when we were allowed outside the walls of the school were guarded like prisoners on leave from a gaol. The only male we ever saw was an ancient gardener, who was not only inexpressibly ugly but was, in Hortense's informed opinion, probably too old to 'do it' (as she put it).

Life was quite extraordinarily dull; lesson followed lesson, day followed day, with a sameness that was so boring as to convince me that nothing in my subsequent life could ever be as uninteresting (an opinion which, happily, life has amply vindicated).

Then one day we saw, with a surprise that quite equalled our anticipatory pleasure, that the old man who normally looked after the heavy garden work, and supervised our own indifferent efforts at cultivation, was absent, and his place supplied for the duration of an illness by his grandson – a young boy of perhaps seventeen, upright and sturdy in appearance, with a mass of curly yellow hair and sturdy shoulders. Four of us were that day working at clearing the weeds from between the rows of cabbages in our garden plots, and we watched from the corners of our eyes as, having removed his shirt, he began to dig the ground not far from us, taking up the last of the crop of potatoes. The sun beat down on his already brown shoulders, and the muscles beneath his skin and the swelling of his thighs and buttocks beneath his tight trousers aroused our keen interest.

I wondered whether perhaps he might be too young to be interested in the pastime which so delighted Hortense's uncle, but she whispered that her uncle had been much of the boy's age [sic] and that we should watch our opportunity. In the end, it was Hortense who contrived that opportunity. The supervising sister was Soeur Rose, and we persuaded Bette – by a combination of threats of violence and the promise of material reward when Eugénie's generous allowance of cakes arrived from home the next week – to lure the good sister into the house for a time by asking her to inspect a sore place which, she said, had developed at the lower part of her belly. As soon as they were gone, Hortense, who naturally took the lead in the enterprise as being most experienced, went up to the boy, whose name was Gaston, and greeted him. I have subsequently learned that it is entirely possible without words to make oneself clear in sensual matters between man and woman, and Hortense must have had a natural command of this instinct even so young, for she had only to lay her hand on the boy's back, and then to withdraw in the direction of the garden hut, for him to follow her quite freely, as if drawn by an invisible line. Eugénie and I followed, closing the door behind us, and placing a sack of grain against it. Almost before we had done that, Hortense was embracing the boy freely, kissing him on the mouth and smoothing his body with her hands. She broke off, threw off her dress with the utmost freedom, and then her drawers, while Gaston's mouth fell open with surprise and remained open with pleasure as she took hold of his trousers – the only garment, as it proved, he now wore – loosened them at the waist and drew them down.

Thus it was that Eugénie and I saw for the first time that part of a man which was to give me (I can say nothing of her) so much pleasure in the years to follow; while it was not, Hortense told me later, the equal of her uncle's, Gaston's tool sprang from his trousers with great readiness, surrounded at the base with fresh-looking blond curls. Eugénie made to push Hortense aside, as being the older, but as Hortense pointed out she was the only one who knew how properly to place herself to receive a man, and it was certain from his confusion, simply standing in the midst of us, that Gaston knew far less. So she threw herself down on a pile of sacks in the corner of the hut, and opened her thighs wide, so the black mark between them was unmistakable. As if in a dream, Gaston knelt between them, and then fell upon her with enthusiasm. In the dark we were unable to see the details of the connection, but Gaston's arse, pure white where the sun had not reached it, began to rise and fall energetically, while Hortense's face, as far as we could see, contorted with pleasure, and we heard her breath coming in short pants.

Within a moment or two, somewhat I thought to Hortense's chagrin, Gaston made a final thrusting motion with his arse and lay still. Eugénie had meanwhile thrown off her clothes and, catching Gaston by the waist, pulled him off Hortense; but when she turned him over, we saw that his tool was drooping and shrunken, and though still somewhat large seemed incapable of working. Eugénie stepped back with a look of anger, but Hortense comforted her by saying that in a moment the matter would be repaired. First wiping him with a corner of her discarded dress, to our great surprise she applied her mouth to the drooping thing, at which Gaston opened his eyes wide and began to watch her with great interest as she moved her lips and tongue about, meanwhile playing with her fingers at the sack beneath. Indeed, as she had promised, within a short time all was as it had been – and it was the turn of Eugénie to lie beneath as Gaston applied himself with no less enthusiasm to demonstrating to her the meaning of love. The pain of which Hortense had spoken did not seem to concern her, and indeed it seems that it was the case that certain mutual experiments she and I had taken in our play had fractured the emblem of maidenhood which should have protected her, and forestalled the pain – a circumstance which I have always thought fortunate, and recommend as advantageous to all educators of young women, who otherwise have to suffer quite unnecessary travail on the occasion of their first making love.

This time Gaston's motions lasted much longer – so long, in fact, that Eugénie had twice called out in pleasure before his eager movements ceased. Impatiently, I caught at his shoulders, and Eugénie wriggled out from beneath him. This time his tool shrank even further; but after all there had been no difficulty before in recovering it to vigour, and I lost no time in applying myself as Hortense had done. Its softness between my lips was both surprising and pleasant; but unfortunately all my endeavours at first had no effect, for it not only refused to grow, but actually declined still further. At my pleading, Eugénie and Hortense also applied themselves, the one joining me in attempting to coax the reluctant member back to life, while the other kissed Gaston's lips and smoothed his chest with her fingers.

At last I felt a stirring between my lips, and a slow growth began; soon, unconciously, Gaston began to thrust his loins upward, and his tool, from being a mere inch or two in length, had grown to five or six, its girth increasing similarly; to feel this growth was a keen pleasure whose interest has never since diminished. Swiftly, I thrust off my clothing, and placed myself on the sacking. Gaston crawled towards me, and I felt his knees pass between my own – when at that moment there was a rattling at the door, and the voice of Soeur Rose was heard calling to us from without.

With an astonishing speed we all thrust our clothes back on, and Gaston pulled on his trousers; and in what seemed less than a minute the door was open and we were somewhat sheepishly withdrawing to the sun and the suspicious eyes of Soeur Rose. She seemed about to comment, as she saw Gaston following us out with a sack of seeds upon his back; but before she could speak, Eugénie asked with emphasis how little Bette's sore spot was, and with such a look that Soeur Rose failed to comment even on the fact that Eugénie and Hortense were unaccountably wearing each other's dresses, while my skirt had a great rent in it through which in my speed I had thrust my foot.

My irritation at being disturbed was extreme – I had been on the edge of a pleasure I had never known, but which Eugénie assured me was quite as great as what Hortense had promised. With what impatience I watched for a chance of leading Gaston to the hut! – an impatience, it seemed, equalled by his own, for he was always catching my eye, and at one time by patting his trousers drew attention to a bulge in them which suggested his eagerness more even than his flashing eye! But we were now watched by Soeur Rose with even more keenness than usual, and soon the opportunity altogether vanished, for the old gardener returned, and we never set eyes on eager Gaston again, though I have no doubt he would have made his way back into the garden had he been able.

The time until I left Boulogne could not have passed too

quickly for me; and though I was reluctant to say goodbye to Hortense and Eugénie, it was with great pleasure that I heard that at the age of seventeen[5] I was to return to England – not indeed to Plymouth, where for one reason or another my mother was not prepared to receive me, but to London, where I was to stay with my maternal grandmother, Mrs Watts, of Covent Garden. There, I was sure, a new life awaited me; and I was ready to greet it with as much vigour as my now strong young body was capable of.

[5] It seems more likely that Emma Crouch returned to England in 1855; in the *Mémoires* she claims then to be 14 years old; actually, she was nearly 18.

CHAPTER TWO

London with grandmother – the gaiety of the West End – an offer of refreshment – Mr Saunders' kindness – Mr Bignell's same – the Argyll Rooms – early instruction – a visit to Paris – a new protector – M. Roubisse engages me – new experience – the artifices of love – I better myself – the Duc de Rivoli

My grandmother was a woman of great kindness, piety, respectability and dullness of character – the height of enjoyment with her was to sit playing at patience while I read to her from a book of travel. She would have liked nothing better than to have apprenticed me to a milliner or dressmaker.[1] But unfortunately as to that intention, she lived in the neighbourhood of the West End of London, an area which despite her best endeavours I determined to explore. If during the day it was a scene of business and energy, at night it became too enticing not to attract a young girl of so forthcoming a nature as my own, especially one deprived of any gaiety or liveliness other than that which may be contrived by a dormitory of young ladies.

No sight in London can surely be as gay as that of Regent Street and the Haymarket at night, with the bright lights of the shop-windows, the cafés, the assembly and concert halls, and the groups of fashionably dressed young women and gentlemen passing to and fro.

My grandmother was forced by my importunity to take me out on several evenings, for she understood that I had no notion of the town life, and while she privately thought

[1] A correspondent claimed in the *Daily News* in 1886 that Emma Crouch spent a brief few weeks in such an apprenticeship.

this a proper state for me, she could not stand out against my pleas. Despite all her attempts to cross the street at the slightest sign of impropriety, she could not disguise from me the nature of the entertainment chiefly offered in the West End, for I was immediately struck by the large number of unaccompanied females of all ages and ranks who inhabited the streets, and who seemed eager to make themselves known to the gentlemen who, on their part, only rarely showed any impatience at being accosted. Some of the women were tall and beautiful, some old, blowsy and filthy; and between the two conditions were those of every sort. Although it was a source of wonder to me how friendly a place was the street (for some young ladies having only for a moment talked to a men, would be offered his arm, sometimes entering a private doorway in Oxenden or Panton Streets, sometimes finding their way to an Oyster Room, or to the Alhambra Music Hall or the Argyll Rooms) I think I was from the first instinctively aware of the nature of the congress.

But, alas! I only glimpsed these delights when, very rarely, my grandmother could be persuaded to venture forth. She watched me with the most attentive eye, and there seemed little chance of escape from her: nor could I contemplate any more permanent escape, since (as I thought) I had no skills which would enable me to depend upon myself for the making of a living.

However, once a week, on Sundays, I would be sent to the church of St Mary-le-Strand attended by Dolly, a peculiarly spiritless servant girl whose task it was to deliver me to the delights of the evening sermon, and then to bring me back. But Dolly, however spiritless, still found more pleasure in the company of a young man who ran a vegetable stall in the nearby market than in the talk of Dr Wyatt, the parson, and it was her habit to see me into the building, and then to go for an evening promenade, only calling for me again when the parson had done. On the fifth such occasion, she was late in her return, and I found myself outside the church door, all the congregation besides having left for their homes. I was not displeased, and began to walk down the street towards Trafalgar Square, my prayer book in my hand. I was after a while conscious of footsteps close behind me, and soon was overtaken by a jocular middle-aged gentleman in an opera cloak, who presently clapped his hand upon my shoulder and asked where I was going.

'To my grandmother's, sir,' was my reply.

'And does you grandmother live near here?'

'Oh, no, sir,' I said (for it was indeed at least five minutes' walk to her house).

'I am sure that a young lady like yourself must be fond of cakes,' said the gentleman, 'and I know of some delicious ones made by a lady who lives not far away. Perhaps I can give you some?'

It was an irresistible offer, for cakes and sweetmeats were not among the pleasures we received at the convent school, nor did my grandmother consider them anything but the tools of the devil to lure young people into a taste for luxury. Besides, the gentlemen, although aged (I imagine he was perhaps forty years old) was slimly built and had a dashing set of just greying whiskers. Down Maiden Lane we walked, past Rule's eating house, and then turned into a dark street behind the Market, where a narrow doorway gave into an equally narrow passage, and then into a small crowded room thick with smoke. Before the cakes he had promised, my new friend ordered up two glasses, and said that I must drink one of them off 'to keep out the cold' (which I thought a strange precaution, for the room was warm enough, nor was the night especially chill). However, I did so. The cakes were then brought, but after one bite I began to feel sick and dizzy.

The gentleman, who now introduced himself as 'Mr Saunders', and said he was a diamond merchant, was extremely upset at my indisposition, and called a young woman who served there, asking if she had perhaps a room where I could lie down. The woman, without seeming surprised at the request, was accommodating enough to provide one, and Mr Saunders helped me upstairs into a back room, and onto a low bed. I was delighted by his kindness, and his care in helping me to loosen my clothing and remove my dress, so that the cool air as he said could help to revive me. I could not swear that I had no notion what he might later require of me; as I have already noted, the bestial side of human nature in general communicates itself without words, and if my new friend did not promise to be of the vigour of young Gaston, nor entirely as prepossessing, being older, neither were Hortense or Eugénie now present to deprive me of my opportunity, and it seemed that at last I might be about to discover the pleasure of lying with someone of the opposite sex.

Alas! to make the story short, my companion, standing over me, had only removed his coat and waistcoat and began to unbutton his shirt, when a second fit of dizziness overcame me, and I fell back senseless on the couch.

I awoke the next morning clad only in my shift, with the most fearful headache and sickness, and a certain soreness below; but not a thing could I remember of any passage that might have occurred between me and Mr Saunders. (I may say that the incident left me with an indescribable aversion to spirits, which I have never since taken.) I hurriedly dressed, and was amazed to find five pounds placed on top of my dress, in the nearby chair.

This was more money than I had ever seen together. I had, moreover, never suspected that payment might enter into any arrangements between the ladies and gentlemen whose relationship I had guessed at; the pleasure alone had always seemed to me to be the motive for their pairing off. But now, I determined that a good income was to be derived from such companionship as Mr Saunders had offered – a greater income, perhaps, than any which the most hardworking milliner could command, and without the hard and dull work such people must endure. I was fully conscious my grandmother would not concur, however, and it was with only slight feelings of unkindness to her that with Mr Saunders' money I rented a room whose grimy window looked down on a corner of the market, and whose single chair, table and cupboard, besides a bed, promised independence rather than luxury.

The keeper of my house was a Mrs Gerard, and the other rooms were almost entirely occupied by gentlemen, one of whom seemed more prosperous than the others; for on the second evening, as I left my room to take a walk, he came out of his room clad in a splendid coat and tall hat, which he swept off to greet me, announcing himself as Mr Robert Bignell.

'I have not had the pleasure of seeing you before,' he said; and when I had introduced myself, and explained that I had but now arrived from France, kindly invited me to the Argyll Rooms, of which he was the proprietor. I have often wondered, since, at the stroke of luck which placed him in my way – or, rather, me in his. It was not to be expected that he should have a room in such a poor house; only that it was convenient to Great Windmill Street, where the Rooms were; and that he preferred, as he said, to save his money rather than to spend it on fripperies.

I had never been in such a place as that to which he now introduced me. On the ground floor was a large dancing room, where the open floor was surrounded by bars for drinking, and above which hung a gallery with velvet-covered benches, on which sprawled young men and women, watching those below, who heatedly engaged in the polka and other gay dances. Mr Bignell kindly accompanied me to a private space in the gallery, and when he had excused himself left me to watch the coloured gathering below, the women in the most expensive and brightly-coloured gowns, with flashing jewellery – much of which, as I was later to learn, was quite sufficiently real to advertise them as expensive properties for whatever men could afford to engage their sympathies.

I sat for an hour watching the dances, when Mr Bignell returned, and gestured me to accompany him, leading the way up to the second floor, along a corridor, and through a door into a low-lit room whose walls were entirely hung in red velvet, floors covered with a luxuriously soft carpet, and – the only piece of furniture in the room – a bed or couch at least eight feet square, covered in large cushions. No sooner than we were in the room, Mr Bignell caught me in his arms and kissed me most violently, with his mouth open and his tongue forcing itself between my lips – a circumstance which at first I was chary of, as being unfamiliar to me, but which I was soon to recognize as a concomitant and mirror of what happens below. He must have felt my inexperience, for he drew back, looked me in the face, and said, half to himself, 'Ah, so that is it!'

'Don't be afraid,' he then said; 'I have nothing to offer you but kindness, if you will offer the same.' Instinctively, I knew what he meant, and lost no time in stripping myself as naked as the day on which I received my first bath at Boulogne. With what pleasure I saw for the first time in Mr Bignell's eyes that pleasure and excitement which a man naturally shows when for the first time he sets eyes on the full beauty of a mistress! I then lay upon the couch, at which he cast many a languishing glance as he removed his own clothing. Unlike that (I would guess) of Mr Saunders, his was a figure infinitely preferable to that of the single man or boy whose nakedness I had previously examined. It had nothing of the immature or girlish about it, though it was white and smooth; his limbs were muscular and sturdy, and from a thicket of black hair between his thighs there rose an engine more massive than poor Gaston's, its fiery tip seeming to burst from its extremity through an imperfectly restraining skin. (It was surprising to me that it was so completely clad, for Gaston's tool had been naked at its end, the skin seeming to fall away – it was of course the difference between circumcision and the natural order which I was now for the first time able to compare.)

Coming towards me, Mr Bignell knelt gently between my legs, bent over, and kissed me again, gradually moving his knees outwards so that my thighs rose above his, and opened so that he was able to slide down between my legs until I felt his tool stiff against my belly. Without any other preliminary, he thrust into me (surprised, as he later confessed, to encounter no obstacle; I was able to explain that my maidenhead had fallen to other girls in play – a circumstance he was never tired of hearing of, so that I had to describe to him in detail the games we played, which astonished him as not being, he was convinced, an occupation which could engage young girls in an English school. I never revealed to him the story of Mr Saunders, as being unlikely to please him, and since it was somewhat a matter of embarrassment to me.)

The moment he was securely within, Mr Bignell began bucking energetically, so that his curls met my own with resounding smacks. I must confess that while I felt my pleasure mounting, I felt there was a certain tenderness lacking – but I put this down (rightly, as it turned out) to over-eagerness, and catching him by the buttocks pulled him with equal enthusiasm into me. In too short a time a shudder went through him, and I felt his organ tighten and relax within me several times, before he ceased thrusting and lay atop of me, panting slightly, with every evidence of pleasure and satisfaction. He kissed me again, and whispered an endearment, before drawing away. He lay at my side, seeming to expect me to do something; and when I showed no sign of movement, pointed to a corner of the room, saying 'Behind the curtain.' I looked at him blankly, when he continued: 'the basin and water'.

When I still showed no sign of understanding, he realized my ignorance, and kindly explained to me that the liquid which he had spilled into me was such as engendered children, and that if I wished to avoid conception I should wash myself thoroughly inside, with soap and water. Of course I did so. I had been entirely ignorant of the consequence of lying with a man, and the engendering of children was equally a mystery to me. Childbearing would undoubtedly have put an end to my new career before it had started, had Mr Bignell not explained matters; and later he was to allow me to bring him to an ecstacy within my hands, so that I could see with my own eyes which I could not understand – that indeed at that moment a liquid came forth with great force from the end of his tool, in which (so he told me) were the invisible creatures which would grow within me into children, if allowed to remain there.

When I had washed and returned to the bed, he asked me the story of my life, and I told him of my education at Boulogne, and said that I had come from there to stay with my grandmother, but who had died a few days ago, leaving me only a few sovereigns, and that I was looking for some post which could supply me with the means of life.

He leant then on one elbow, running his finger from my shoulder down to the tip of one breast, and remarked that he believed I possessed talents which would make it unnecessary for me to indulge in menial work. Modesty forbids that I should repeat his praises of my figure and likelihood; suffice it to say that his mere observation of them brought him to a new expectation, for I saw his tool begin again to grow, as Gaston's had done, if rather more slowly – so that falling to my knees I took it between my lips, at the same time taking his stones between my fingers and gently fumbling them. He took this for a natural willingness in me rather than experience, and with the utmost pleasure sprang fully to life, and raising me threw me upon the bed, placed my thighs over his shoulders, and himself began to moisten and tickle me with his tongue, while his fingers teased my nipples to such intense hardness that they quite pained me.

Within the next half hour I realized for the first time the meaning of true sensual pleasure, as far removed from the childish experiments at Boulogne as the throne is set above a beggar's chair! If Mr Bignell found me at first an ignorant pupil, he found me I think a quick one; and also I began to discover in myself an equal capacity for enjoyment both of the emotions roused in me by an attentive lover, and of the joys I was capable of giving. I realized too what every lover wishes, to be capable of giving the utmost pleasure to a woman; and if on this occasion, as ecstacy followed ecstacy almost to the extent of irritation, I had by no means to counterfeit, one of the most important lessons to be learned by a lady who intends to devote her life to these pleasures is that she must either be capable of invariably enjoying the delights of love, or more likely be the finest actress off the boards.

Fortunately, nature has made me the happiest of receivers of sensual pleasure; and fortunately, too, the mode of life I have enjoyed has enabled me to teach the gentlemen who have come to me much about the art of love – indeed, I have heard from many sources that wives and mistresses alike have had cause to thank me for the early lessons I have read their husbands in that book.

But I digress. It was long past midnight before Mr Bignell

and I, bathed in the dews of our excesses, had exhausted our bodies in the pursuit of that heavenly throbbing of our mutual blisses; whereupon he had to remove and dress himself to look to the shutting of the doors of the Rooms, while he gave me permission to remain where I was, and then, showing me a suite of rooms next to that in which we had been engaged, told me that I was to regard them as my own! – upon which I sent an extra guinea to Mrs Gerard and forsook her house.

Mr Bignell had, he told me, at first been a bootmaker, then a tobacconist in Piccadilly, where he had made enough money to buy into the Rooms with two partners. By the time I met him, these two, Mr Laurent and Mr Bryer, were very much in the background, and Mr Bignell was talking of buying them out (which indeed he was to do a few years later, eventually to die in his own house in Kew, leaving a fortune of £20,000. But that is no part of my story.)

Mr Bignell was madly my lover. He had, as he told me, passages with several ladies, all of whom undertook to make love on a business footing, and his main attention in discovering whom was (he said) to ensure that they could properly assuage the passions of other gentlemen coming to the Rooms. He had at first thought of me in that light, he confessed; but my natural gifts and innocence combined with my young appearance, which were of the greatest excitement to him, persuaded him to be my only lover, and completely engaged his heart.

For some months we were blissfully happy. It was an education to me to watch the crowds in the Rooms, always so well-behaved (on which Mr Bignell insisted) though of all conditions; and watching the ladies and gentlemen pairing off to retire to a 'private room' (the best of which was that in which we had had our first passage of love) or leaving for some previously arranged rendezvous, brought me often to the pitch of sensuality, which ensured that when Mr Bignell was able to retire with me our mutual flame burned as fierily as on that first night.

On Sundays, when the Rooms were closed, we often excursed to the country in a hired carriage, leaving it at some inn to walk through the fields and woods, and on more than one occasion in the warmth of the summer sun were so overtook by our passions that we made love beneath some hedge or in some copse, quite in the manner of the bumpkins, before retiring to the inn for supper, and then tired to our bed.

At other times, I was at liberty to look about me, and since it was already an idea of mine that I might at some time wish or need to move more generally in the world, I examined those women – of whom there were many – who seemed to have a bent for living by their wits. It was soon clear to me that those who were most successful were those who, while they might please many men, had at one time one chief protector. The others, who relied solely on any man whose attention they could command for a single night or a single hour, very soon, or so it seemed to me, became poor and degraded.

Of the first class, I soon got to know several, some of whom were kept by wealthy members of the aristocracy, or perhaps men of business, in villas at Richmond or at Epping or in Regent's Park. Of the second, the so-called *prima donnas*, the most successful relied on a few – perhaps four or six – men to keep them, and these they would meet at the Rooms or the Portland Rooms, or perhaps at Kate Hamilton's, where only men prepared to spend six or eight pounds or more in an evening were allowed entry. Some of them spent their afternoons in the Burlington Arcade, in small rooms which they rented above the most innocent businesses. From the windows they would signal to passing gentlemen, who for the most part were on the look out for, and perfectly understood, those signals, and who would slip past the millinery wares or the displays of jewellery to make their way up narrow staircases to narrow couches on which with these ladies (mostly professing to be governesses or the daughters of poor clergymen) they could for a guinea or less satisfy their itches.

Although these ladies often made in excess of £20 or £30 in a week, these sums represented the utmost of their capabilities. I was determined to do better, which I had no doubt could be done by the simple expedient of organization; young I was, but not too young to see that the best I could hope from mere prostitution was a genteel poverty at the best, and at the worst disease and death.

It was in March of 1858 that Mr Bignell came to me with a piece of paper in his hand: it was a passport for Paris, made out to 'Mr Robert Bignell travelling with his wife'. When we arrived there he took me straight to the Hôtel de Lille et d'Albion in the Rue St Honoré, where a suite of rooms was engaged, and thence it was that he showed me the city with which I instantly fell in love.

We were there a month, after which time Mr Bignell announced that he had to return to London. But by then my love for my new city had outweighed even my gratitude to that gentleman; and I being confident of my being able to make a living for myself there announced I would rather remain behind. There was, of course, a painful scene, for he was determined that I should return with him. In turn, he abused and made love to me, even proposing that he should marry me. In the end, driven mad by his insistence, I seized the passport from his desk and threw it into the fire. At which he seized me, tore the clothes from my body, and began to beat me. Then in passion he turned another way, and with the utmost violence he threw me upon the bed and himself upon me, not even pausing to remove his clothes. It was then I learned the final lesson he was to teach me: that pleasurable though the delights of the smoothest amorous congress may be, there are delights also in violence. We tore at each other's flesh like wild things, and only refrained from our passion after an hour, panting like exhausted animals.

'Well, Emma,' he said to me, 'I suppose that we must part. You know where I am to be found when you return to London, as return you will. My mistake was to love you, but I am cured of that.' Whereupon he left me a handsome present, and made off for Calais, leaving me to look about me and make my plans. And ambitious plans they were, but they did not include a return to London, nor was I to see that place again for many years.

In the first place, I must find a new protector. The money Mr Bignell had left me, while generous enough, was not enough to keep me at the Hôtel de Lille, nor was I looking to beg my living in the gutter. Dressing myself with care on the very evening of his departure, I made forth into the streets, and taking a glass of wine sat at a table outside one of the cafés of the Rue St Honoré. Within an hour, a young man approached me and asked permission to buy me a drink. He was, as I discovered later that night, not the aristocrat for whom I had hoped, but an officer in the French navy – a fact which might have dissuaded me from his company had I known of it, for my recollection of the manners of sailors from my earliest years were not of the happiest. But d'Amenard, contrary to what I might have expected, was kind and loving, and while he had (he told me) been without female company since his ship had left Barbados many months before, he was the gentlest and most considerate of lovers. Later, I was to express my surprise at his lack of urgency, whereupon he admitted that he, like most of his companions, made use of the ship's boys for a convenience during long voyages – a thing which the boys expected and rarely refused. On my telling him I could not know what he meant, or how a boy could be used for such a purpose, he explained at length to me, and even offered a demonstration, which I declined (on which he laughed, saying there was no need, but that some men desired even to treat a lady in that way, though he himself did not).

d'Amenard took me to rooms in a mean house in the Rue des Bluets, now torn down – not as satisfactory even as Mrs Gerard's, the walls being so thin that the shouts and cries of those in neighbouring rooms continually disturbed us (upon which d'Amenard would be as loud as possible in his enjoyment of me, 'to spread the news about', as he called it). He explained that his family lived in a small village called Nans-les-Pins, some sixty kilometres from Paris, but that he had fallen out with them and had been disallowed their society, whereupon he had taken these rooms as a temporary expedient. I suspect that he hoped, too, for livelier company than a small village could afford. In a month he had again to take ship, and I was sorry to see the amiable buffoon go, though he had scarcely provided for me as well as Mr Bignell, nor was ever likely to do so. However, he had provided somewhere for me to remove my things to, from the Hôtel, and a day or two before his departure, while he had been out seeking a berth (his money being exhausted) I had been talking to one of the girls who shared the house, and who though now in middle years, had obviously once been handsome. She had given me an introduction to a certain Roubisse, who she felt sure could 'use me'. The idea of being 'useful' to someone else, in the way of business, did not attract me, but by now I had determined that I needed a protector of more generous means than poor d'Amenard, and so on the day after the latter left, I made my way to a house in the Rue

Débarcadère, and there found M. Roubisse, who received me in a well-furnished office, where he sat behind a desk like a man of business.

I had sent him a message as to my means of introduction to him, and he made short work of telling me what would be required of me: *viz* that I should hold myself ready to go off with whatever gentleman he should procure for me, and be kind to him, for which I would receive a certain sum.

'But first,' he said, 'there remains a formality.' At which he rang a bell, and into the room came a tall and handsome youth whom he introduced to me as M. Delamarche, whose task it was to examine the quality of the ladies to be placed by M. Roubisse on what he termed 'his list'.

I followed the youth through an inner door to a comfortable room, where a bed was the chief article of furniture and, realizing what was expected of me, I was as naked as M. Delamarche within an instant. By now, I felt that I had had considerable experience of love; yet it was clear to me soon enough that M. Delamarche, whatever his years, had much, much more. He insisted, for instance, that I should prepare myself for him by frigging myself energetically while he looked on (a circumstance which I found sufficiently embarrassing, having believed hitherto that it was a private activity; but M. Delamarche assured me that it was something many gentlemen enjoyed observing, and later tutored me in the postures to adopt meanwhile). Then it was his desire that I should kneel before him and minister to him with my lips, while placing the index finger of one hand up his fundament, which appeared to please him.

When, after this, we laid upon the bed, it was (for the first time, again, in my experience) not in the normal fashion, but head to tail, so that while his member was within reach of my lips, his tongue was able to busy itself with me – this, he informed me, was a position known in his country as the *soixante-neuf*, or sixty-nine, from the resemblance of those figures to a representation of our posture.

By this time my interest in these new experiences was secondary to my excitement, for he was, though no doubt himself regarding our congress as a matter of business, by no means immune to enjoyment; and as a final surprise, he insisted that I should place myself over him, crouching so that I could lower myself upon his upright tool, which seemed to sink in me to my very navel, and then instructed me to move myself up and down upon my heels, until his own bucking and leaping like a horse between my thighs indicated that he had come off. Whereupon he roused himself upon his elbows and kissed me energetically upon both breasts, announcing that 'he thought I would do'.

'I'm not sure, however,' he added, 'what M. Roubisse will think.' He then girt himself with a towel, and left the room, returning to announce that M. Roubisse thought I had great promise, but that I was insufficiently knowledge-able to be despatched to a real *connoisseur*; he, M. Delamarche, was to undertake my further education. And so I was given a room in the house, and for the next two weeks came daily to that same couch, where I was instructed in every posture, gesture and lascivious trick. I never succeeded in discovering how M. Delamarche, whose age must have been no more than twenty-five, came to be in the position he held in M. Roubisse's business, any more than I discovered how the latter had built up his business (something of keen interest to me).

It was clear the latter had nothing to do with any of the ladies on his list, for I never saw one of them come to the house, nor did M. Roubisse ever make the slightest overture to myself. At the end of my stay there, when I had been told that my tutorage was complete, I raised the matter with M. Delamarche. He smiled, went with me to the door of M. Roubisse's office, knocked, and when there was no reply, opened the door and ushered me in. The room was empty. Delamarche went across to a cupboard behind the desk, and opened the door, beckoning to me. I followed him, and there saw, within the cupboard, a window giving into the room where we had just been! From the other side, the glass was that of a mirror set just above the couch, still warm from our farewell jousting of half an hour ago! I blushed to think of the many times I had caught my own eye in that mirror, my face flushed and damp with the perspiration of lascivious enjoyment. Watching couples at play, M. Delamarche explained, was M. Roubisse's *marquer*. I must confess that this was somewhat repugnant to me, and has remained so; I have of course admitted men to positions from which they could watch me in congress with another man, but the fact that they should take pleasure in such a fleshless activity remains a wonder.

However that may be, my fortnight at school with M. Delamarche was a happy one as well as profitable: from him I learned not only many physical practices, but some others; how for instance to counterfeit an ecstacy when I had not one, how to raise a man from the dead in more than one way, what wine was best for arousal and which best to send a man to sleep, how to use perfumes to enhance the act, and other arts to diminish it. (A certain pressure at the root of risen manhood will for instance almost certainly result in the toppling of the tower – a useful artifice when men are too quick to spend, for otherwise they become impatient at parting with the sum which earlier they had been all too quick to disburse. Greed is not only an unbecoming but in the end an unprofitable trait in my profession.)

I left M. Roubisse's house with no regrets except saying goodbye to my good friend M. Delamarche. He was careful, loving and tender as a lover (except when demonstrating some of the harsher aspects of love), and I believe that he found me amiable as well as a quick study. However, I did not delude myself that he held me in especial esteem; and indeed when, having said farewell to M. Roubisse, I went from his office to the inner room to say a final farewell to his good officer, I opened the door to find the latter already mounted between the thighs of a slender black Moorish girl, from which position he lifted a hand in acknowledgement. (This was the first black girl I ever saw naked; it was I believe an experiment on M. Roubisse's part, his having been brought the girl by a merchant who had had her imported for his use from Africa. But I believe he must have been unable to convince his clients of her acceptability, for I never heard of a black girl who had a success of this sort in society.)

I now returned to rooms of my own, not in the Rue des Bluets, but far better ones in the Place du Havre, which had been taken for me by M. Roubisse with money to be returned by me in due course.

It was speedily returned, for I had the knack of pleasing the customers he sent me, who not only paid the sum he asked of them, but continually left me presents of my own, with which in due time I was able to move to better and better rooms – to the Rue Lepeletier and then the Rue Grande Batelière. From the first I treated my business *as* a business, keeping for instance a ledger in which I entered all the names and descriptions of my lovers, together with details of their families, and of course more personal details; so that not only was I able to greet them in the form they preferred – perhaps completely naked beneath a *peignoir*, or clad in underclothing of various sorts, or more eccentrically (in the case of one gentleman, for instance, in only a pair of riding-boots and a short leather topcoat) – but later was able to enquire by name about the health of their wives and daughters or the progress of their affairs.

At last the time came when I wished to dispense with the services of M. Roubisse. One of my fellow employees warned me that he would never let me go, once contracted to him; and I prepared for battle. But by great good luck, not long before I was decided to approach him, news came that he had been found dead, his heart having given out, it seems, while he was seated before his window watching as M. Delamarche performed the usual tests with a new girl. The latter retired from the business, or at least from its management in Paris, and left the city, and I was free. This was six years after my leaving Mr Bignell; a long enough time, and tedious enough often, but one during which I laid the foundations of a fortune. I had much for which to thank M. Roubisse, however large the profit he made from me, for it was almost the last customer he sent me who aided my real rise in the profession.

One day I received a message that a certain 'Jean' would wait upon me at midday. At that hour, a tall, slim youth of twenty-five presented himself. I knew him as 'Jean' for a week or two, during which time he became besotted with me. I learned later that I was the first professional woman he had lain with, his experience up to then having been with amateurs whose lips were made only for sipping tea. After declaring himself determined never to part from me, he revealed himself as no common young man, but as Victor Massena, third Duc de Rivoli,[2] and the distinguished grandson of the famous Marshal of Napoléon I.

---

[2] Later fifth Prince of Essling, 1836–82. Their liaison lasted for five years.

CHAPTER THREE

The birth of 'Cora Pearl' – Carole Hassé – low entertainment – frustration – the Prince de Ponte Corvo – his gift – my acknowledgement – his education – cherchez la femme – departure of the Prince – the Duc Citron – the Duc de Morny – La Souris Blanche – masked balls – accepted in society – life at the Château de Beauséjour – Mongolian attitudes – the Garden of Eden and its rules

Upon leaving M. Roubisse's protection, I had moved my apartments yet again, this time to a house at 61 Rue de Ponthieu, which I shared with a friend, Mlle Carole Hassé, and where I passed for the first time under the name of 'Cora Pearl', which I venture to believe I have made famous not only in Paris but throughout Europe.

Mlle Hassé was not, I confess, so much a friend that I would under other circumstances have engaged her as a partner. She was a young lady of about my own age, but of a less refined ambition, who had grown up in Alsatia and still retained the strong accent with which she spoke when she first learned French. I had, on the other hand, by now achieved some finesse in that language – though from time to time I still found it advantageous to simulate an English, or even a Devonshire or a Cockney accent, for just as in London the acme of perfection in a mistress is that she should have come from Paris, so in Paris it is the fashion to have an English mistress, who some men prefer to be of a somewhat coarse disposition.

Caro's success might have been the result of her being indeed coarse in other ways than speech. She furnished her rooms almost in the manner of a public brothel – and her bed was dressed in black sheets, upon which her big white body looked like that of some stranded dead fish. However, it would be vain to deny that her rough but haughty manner was not appealing [*sic*] to some men, and later she was to become the favourite of the Comte de Maugny, and to set herself up almost in rivalry to myself. For the time of which I speak, however, we conducted ourselves as friends and associates, and were able to entertain gentlemen together when the occasion demanded.

It was at the Rue de Ponthieu that I first tasted the real luxury which a consistent and generous income can afford, partly due to the generosity of the Duc de Rivoli, whose fortune was such that he could afford to lavish money upon me without apparent diminution of his stock. I have to confess that it was money easily earned, for Massena was a lazy man whose indolence was such that his most passionate act was to climb upon me and discharge himself with as little effort as possible. This would have been tedious in some men, but Massena's charm and gallantry (not to speak of his generosity) were such that one could forgive him anything. He liked me to accompany him to the opera and the theatre and on public occasions, and to be dressed as befitted a companion of his; and since he had no notion of the cost of clothes or even jewellery, I was able to obtain from him ten and twenty times the money which I would have been able to persuade from a more careful man.

So it was that I was able to acquire my great chef Salé, who came to me from a household so distinguished that even after a passage of years I had better not divulge it; he was happy to cook for myself and the Duc, or for a party of thirty people, and it was not always true that the latter party would necessarily be more expensive than the former.

While Massena was always happy to be present at large

parties at the Rue de Ponthieu, and to watch while Caro and some of her low friends entertained the gentlemen with dancing and charades which had in common only the utmost coarseness, he made it clear that I was not to entertain other gentlemen to the charms of my person while under his protection. Since his own activities in the bedchamber were not especially passionate, and since I had now for some time been accustomed to enjoy a rather high level of sensual attention, I soon became extremely irritated by his lack of attention to my beauty. And it was just when that deficiency was most keenly felt that the Duc himself introduced me, at the Opéra, to the Prince Achille Murat.[1]

The Prince was the second son of Napoléon Lucien Charles Murat, Prince de Ponte Corvo, and an American lady. He had been born in the United States of America, where he was brought up in straitened circumstances. With the establishment of the Empire, however, circumstances had much improved for the family, which now, with an inheritance restored, kept up town houses in the Avenue Montaigne and the Rue Jean-Goujon. Prince Achille had his own establishment in the Rue Presbourg.

At our first meeting, it seemed to me that the young Prince eyed me with rather more admiration than was strictly wise in the presence of an older protector. We talked of hunting, and I mentioned my intention at some time to set up a stable. Imagine my surprise when on the following day a beautiful chestnut mare was delivered to me, with the Prince's card! Of course I called upon him that afternoon in order to express my thanks.

The young man – he was only seventeen years of age at this time – received me in a handsome masculine sitting-

[1] 1847–95.

room,[2] where the chairs and couches were furnished in green leather, and the walls bore portraits of his ancestors and relatives, most of them with lowering features. Murat was dressed in a long, heavy dressing-gown of red velvet, and bowed to me somewhat severely. However, when his footman had left the room, he beckoned me to sit by him on a couch, and refused to let me speak of my thanks for his gift. He was a handsome youth, his upper lip only marked by a faint moustache, and his dark eyes had something of a look of innocence about them.

I was in somewhat of a confusion about the extent to which I should offer my thanks, but also, it must be said, more than a little disturbed by the presence of such an attractive young man at a period when my only lover was less than commonly attentive. Fortunately we had only exchanged a few polite phrases when he seized my hand, kissed it, and began professing his adoration. It was now clear to me what form he expected my gratitude to take, if not under the actual name of gratitude; and nothing loath I placed his hand upon my bosom and slipped it down inside my dress so that it held my breast, whereupon he began feverishly to kiss me and to run his other hand up the length of my leg.

I never learned of the Prince the extent of his previous amorous adventures, but either they had been keener than his years and aspect suggested, or his instinct for the arts of love was more than commonly sharp, for within five minutes he had shed his dressing-gown (under which he wore only a pair of drawers beneath which a powerful manhood betrayed itself), and had undressed me to my shift; whereupon, with difficulty it seemed, he drew back, and offering me his hand led me into the next room, where a bed awaited us upon which, taking me in his arms with

[2] at 7, Rue Presbourg.

more strength than a youth of his age might seem to possess, he softly laid me, then drawing my shift over my head and removing his drawers, set to work in earnest.

There is ever a special delight in teaching the arts of love to the young, and in all my passages in that most enjoyable of pastimes, those I remember with the keenest pleasure have been in just such cases, for however much pleasure the attentions of a practised lover may give to a woman whose profession might tend to make her jaundiced in the art, there is a peculiar pleasure in instructing a young man in subtleties of which he has hitherto been ignorant.

That Prince Achille's previous adventures had been with servants and the like cannot be doubted, for he placed himself between my legs without preliminary and busied himself with gaining entry with all the simplicity of a dog with a bitch. However, his figure was so slight that strong though he was I was able by placing my hands on his shoulders to turn him upon his back and pin him there with my superior weight, kissing him the while to still his protests. Surprise then kept him quiet as I traced with my tongue the line of his neck, then moved downward to his paps, the little springy black hairs around them the only ones to decorate the platform of his chest, teasing each one so that the tiny nipple became like an orange pip beneath my tongue. I could feel him shiver with pleasure as he realized for the first time that the art of love as I practised it had more to offer than the welcoming of his tool by my own tender part.

After a while, I moved yet further down, my tongue making a snail's trace down his belly, pausing to thrust into that delightful knot, his navel, and then yet lower, whence black curls marked a broad path to his tool, now hard as ivory and as white, that had almost bruised my breasts as it sprang between them. He began to make little movements with his loins, as though to thrust himself at me; yet I ignored this, and simply feeling his upright instrument soft on my cheek, passed it by and kissed the tops of his thighs, where still there was only the faintest mat of hairs, which I caught between my lips; then parting his thighs placed myself between them, lifting his stones so that I could caress each one with my tongue, even pressing them with my lips, before finally running my tongue up his instrument and parting my lips to slip it between them.

I knew that as with most inexperienced lovers, the pleasure of this was too keen to be long maintained. As my lips passed over the knob of his tool, and I tickled with my finger the part between his balls and fundament, I felt his whole body quiver, and before I had drawn my lips more than three or four times up the shaft, he roughly threw me off – a politeness which spoke of his natural tenderness and concern as well as of his inexperience – as the convulsion came, and ample proof of his passion exuded from him with the celerity and force of a shot from a gun!

He seemed speechless as he bent over to kiss me, then wiping his body with the sheets before drawing me up to lie with him, embraced me tenderly and with many endearments. So resilient is youth that before his tool had seemed to shrink at all, it began to recover its strength, and this time I did not object as he slipped between my thighs and entered me, for the pleasure of bringing him off had brought me to a pitch of eagerness almost matching his own. Still, his passion was such that he was finished almost before I began; but again youth recovered him speedily, and for the rest of the afternoon our pleasure was mutual, for three more times he roused himself, and for the two final attacks was able to maintain himself for such a time as allowed me to the ample happiness he himself was experiencing.

It was now the time at which the Duc would be coming to call at the Rue de Ponthieu, and so I rose and dressed,

while the Prince lay naked upon the bed in happy exhaus-
tion, his adoring looks speaking of his gratitude while the
limp prostration of his manhood told of the utmost
satisfaction. So I took my leave of him, though not without
protestations of renewing the pleasure of his acquaintance.

Certainly that pleasure was renewed, for although Rivoli
was so kindly and civilized a person that it was impossible
for me to break with him without pain (and it is also true
that the contribution he made to the upkeep of my
establishment was valuable), I swiftly became so devoted to
Murat that his company was quite indispensable to me.
With his help, the stables of the house in the Rue de
Pontheiu were indeed soon established – during the five
years after I met Murat, I bought over sixty of the finest
horses, which were cared for by a number of English
grooms (though of course at one time I rarely had more
than a dozen). I was able to persuade Rivoli to allow me the
expense of buying some, and Murat's advice in the choos-
ing of them and additional contributions to their purchase
showed splendid results.

This may sound like extravagance; yet it is not so. I was
after all by the middle of the decade one of the most
celebrated of those ladies some wit described as *les grandes
horizontales*: of a hundred thousand women in the city who
devoted their lives to love, there were scant few who had
attached themselves to protectors of such wealth that they
were able to live as richly as the wife of any aristocrat.
Marie Colombier, Blanche d'Antigny, Adèle Courtois,
Anna Deslion and a few others joined me in being seen at
the best balls, at the race meetings at Baden (where however
only I was permitted the honour of driving my carriage into
the Enclosure[3]) and in the company of many a prince and
duke.

[3] Actually, another courtesan, Hortense Schneider, shared that honour.

The Duc de Rivoli did not express himself as enthusiastic when he heard, as various 'friends' soon made sure that he did hear, of my meetings with Prince Achille; and that young man was not the most tactful of creatures. When my two lovers met – as meet they often must in the small world of Parisian aristocracy – there was at best a cold silence, and at worst an exchange of which the young man almost always got the best. For instance, when in the company of some other people both Duc and Prince were joining in a general conversation about the growing lassitude of an elderly member of the Government, the Duc remarked: '*Cherchez le femme!*' 'Ah, but *monsieur le duc*,' the Prince responded, 'you know very well that I have already found her.' The Duc immediately made an excuse and left the room.

For a period of time, however, I was happily able to continue to amuse my dear Duc, while at the same time tasting with the Prince the pleasures to which the former was not so strongly addicted. That happy state of affairs ended when, in 1865, a fellow from whom I had bought two carriage horses had the impertinence to send me a bill for several thousand francs which I had already paid him. Since I had no record of my payment, Murat was kind enough to sign a document stating that he had seen me pay the man. An evil journalist, Henri Rochefort,[4] long an enemy of the Napoléons, attacked the Prince in the press, and the latter was forced to challenge him. Murat winged the vicious fellow, but the damage was done, and he had to leave for Africa on the Emperor's instructions (who paid his outstanding debts).

I supped with the Prince and his father on the eve of his departure. The old man sat with us so long after supper that we were both in an extreme excess of longing,

[4] by birth, Comte Victor Henri de Rochfort-Luçay.

exacerbated rather than relieved by Murat's stretching out his foot to caress the inside of my thigh as I sat conversing with his father about music and cookery. Though the old man eventually fell asleep at the table, there was little we could do but frig ourselves to an irritable satisfaction before he woke and demanded that his son take him home. And so I parted with the Prince, whose many promises of a final gift came to nothing, though from his father I received, some days later, the gift of an eighty-piece silver dinner service and a gold watch.

Rivoli, dissatisfied with the attentions I paid Murat, had by now cooled somewhat in his devotion, but fortunately I was introduced by the English Lord Henry Seymour to an acquaintance of his whom to tease me he introduced simply as the Duc Citron. This was the name given to Prince William of Orange, the heir of the King of Holland, by his friend the British Prince of Wales. Orange was a weak-faced, plump man, jovial without being spirited, and excessively dull in conversation. From him I received even less amorous satisfaction than from Rivoli, and although he remained a friend for some time, I received only a moderate contribution to the upkeep of my establishment, although he did give me one beautiful pearl necklace, long enough for him (in a rare display of imagination) to lay not around my neck but around my waist. However, soon a patron of more formidable proportions was to offer himself.

One morning in December of 1864, I was skating in the Bois when I was greeted by a man whose face and figure I had often seen on great occasions. 'Cora Pearl skating!' he exclaimed – 'a strange meeting of fire and ice!' I responded, 'M. le Duc, since you have so neatly broken the ice, may we perhaps share a drink?' And so it was that I found myself taking champagne with M. le Duc de Morny,[5] the half-

[5] 1811–65, the illigitimate son of Queen Hortense of Holland and Comte de Flahaut de Billarderie. He organized his brother's *coup d'état* in 1851.

brother and heir of the Emperor, son of Queen Hortense, and a man so rich that no-one has ever succeeded in even approximately estimating the extent of his fortune.

The day after we met, a splendid white Arab horse arrived at my stables, followed shortly afterwards by Morny himself. I had had a small riding-school constructed next to the stables, and told one of my grooms to take the Duc there, for I would like to show off the horse's paces. I had by now become a good horsewoman,[6] always having had, I suppose, a natural aptitude for riding; now, I quickly stripped off my clothes (happily, it was late spring, and a warm day!) and shortly rode that Arab steed into the riding-school to present to Morny the spectacle of an unadorned Pearl upon the back of as fine a piece of horseflesh as there was in Paris. Incidentally, the absence of skirts conduces to a more perfect understanding between horse and rider than can possibly be obtained when many folds of clothing prevent the loins of the rider from feeling the instinctive reactions of the steed, and the steed from appreciating the slightest promptings of the rider. Gentlemen, who commonly ride in close-fitting breeches, know this well; ladies, less so.

After putting the horse through several motions, I drew up before the Duc. He stepped forward to take the reins, as though to help me dismount; but to ensure that his fever was not too promptly abated, I said: 'No, sir, just as a horse needs care after exercise, so I need to bathe and rest. But be assured that your gift will be acknowledged by my lasting admiration.' Whereupon I wheeled about and rode into the stables.

Next day, I naturally received an invitation to de Morny's house, where I was escorted past an immense pack of

[6] Nestor Roqueplan, of *Figaro*, described Cora Pearl as riding 'with unequalled distinction and skill'. She is said to have spent 30,000 francs in three years with one horsedealer alone.

petitioners waiting to plead for ʔid of one kind and another, and taken to a private room where he was waiting. He was a tall, slender man much of whose hair had unfortunately gone, but with a fine moustache and small, pointed beard, given to tickling. He was very elegant, and with much charm and grace and vigour, as well without his clothes as with them. Not to be tedious, that was proved to me amply upon that first visit, when he proved as eager to please as to be pleased. I became not only his mistress (of whom he had many) but his friend (of whom he had few), and the friend too of his wife, the Princess Sophie, a natural daughter of the Emperor Alexander of Russia.

The Princess brought great gaiety and brilliance to Paris, with her wonderful sense of dress. Many found her 'difficult', for indeed she did not suffer fools gladly. She was in some ways still a child, ready to express her every feeling with spirit, and without necessarily the deference which some might have felt due to those older than herself. She was very pretty, small and with very fair hair (hence her nickname, *La Souris Blanche* (the White Mouse). She was very slim, with little hands, dark eyes, a sharp nose. On one of the first occasions when I was with her in public, at a fancy dress ball, she dressed as one of the elements, Air, in a light gown with floating streamers of gauze in blue and white. When her dance was over, she sat with me to watch the rest; but the Duc de Dino, dressed as a tree with much greenery, sat in front of us, so that we could not see. I was annoyed, but said nothing; the Princess, however, simply struck him upon the trunk with her tiny feet, and exclaimed '*Otez-vous de là!*',[7] and when he still did not move, seized him by the branches and tried to throw him to the ground. Failing in this, she sat muttering imprecations to herself for the rest of the evening.

---

[7] 'Get away out of it!'

Although they showed no signs of discord before me, I believe that Morny's life with his wife had its rough moments; certainly I attended more than one party at which she simply refused to be present, because of some caprice, and he had to receive and entertain his guests alone. I was fond of them both, however, though I knew them only for a year – during which time the Duc was generous enough to enable me to rent, late in 1864, the Château de Beauséjour,[8] near Orléans, as a country home.

It was through the Duc, too, that I met a great many members of society, of which he had always been a leader, notably through his many parties and masked balls (most of which, alas, took place before I knew him). He is said to have invented, in modern times, the idea of the masked ball, at which M. Fould, Rouher, Comtesse Walewska and Comtesse le Hon, the wife of the Belgian Ambassador, invariably wore the most luxurious and expensive disguises. The Marquis de Gallifet, too, an eccentric young man who delighted in outraging public opinion, usually appeared in some strange guise – once as an apothecary with an enema about his neck! Another time, he appeared as the owner of a peep-show, with a large box with a peep-hole in it. The ladies crowded round craving a peep; when they looked, there inside the box, every limb and feature realistically delineated and articulated, were two tiny figures in ivory engaged in making love.

The Duc was also known to take advantage of such occasions for his own purpose. Once, he disappeared from the public rooms in the company of a certain lady, and both were absent for some time. When they reappeared, it was noticed that he no longer wore the collar of the Légion d'Honneur around his neck, but that, without the lady's

---

[8] which she later bought.

knowledge, it was now hanging among the frills of her petticoats!

I was by now able to spend a great deal of money in maintaining myself as a lady, for my attachment to de Morny (never slow to advertise his latest acquisition, whether horse- or woman-flesh) had resulted in a natural elevation of the value of the presents given to me by those gentlemen who wished to pay me (to be frank) their tribute. I was also by now accepted wherever I wished to go in society; de Morny had made sure of that. On one occasion an underling had the impertinence to refuse me entry into the rooms at Baden, whereupon the Duc, hearing of it, sent me a note summoning me to meet him at the casino, and offering me his arm escorted me into the rooms, presenting me with a large purse to hazard at the tables.

Both in town and in the country it was my custom to entertain well. Salé was given free rein to purchase whatever he needed – and I may say that the expense was considerable: on one occasion the kitchen bill was for 30,000 francs in one fortnight. On the other hand, while I have always declined to discuss money in public, I may say that the rumour that at this time the normal gift left by a gentleman after spending the night with me was 12,000 francs[9] is not without foundation.

The gardens at the Château, running down to the river, would in summer be full of gentlemen and their companions – and it was rarely that at weekends twenty or thirty guests were not present. Those were high-spirited times. Young men have always been fond of horse-play, and some of the games they played were rougher and more heartless than others. One, of which I am still somewhat ashamed, concerned the local doctor,[10] a middle-aged man

[9] Certainly not less than £8,000 in today's currency.
[10] In the *Mémoires* Cora Pearl tells this story of a highranking State official, and sets it in her Paris house.

of considerable size who had been paying his court to me ever since I took the Château. He was so self-assured, so pompous, so boring, that I was persuaded to play a cruel trick on him: that is, to pretend to yield to his blandishments, and to make an appointment to meet him in my rooms. He came, eager for the fray, and needed no persuasion to undress, whereupon I informed him that the service I requested of him if he was to enjoy me was that he should go down on all fours and allow me to ride him round the room. While we were in full canter, my slipper acting as a whip and my steed in a beastly state of eagerness, fourteen or fifteen male guests appeared from the next door rooms, and the poor doctor was laughed quite out of countenance and, visibly wilting, was chased from the room and into the garden where, upon my throwing down his clothes to him from the window, he hurriedly dressed and made off. I did however make the others swear never to let the news of his discomfiture be known in the village, and as far as I know, it never was.

On another occasion, the fun was more innocent, and to my mind more amusing. Comte Albert de Maugny, joining a party at the Château one weekend in summer, had brought me a present – copies of a set of prints from Mongolia depicting a warrior and a concubine enjoying each other on horseback.[11]

The Comte humorously offered to wager 20,000 francs that these scenes were impossible to counterfeit. He had chosen the wrong person with whom to enter such a wager, and I had soon persuaded Captain Deschamps, of the French Artillery (whom I knew to be both an excellent horseman and a dogged and persistent lover) to essay the acrobatics with me. The house guests assembled in a

[11] A scroll containing such scenes, painted by an anonymous eighteenth century Mongolian artist, exists in the collection of the Gichner Foundation for Cultural Studies in Washington, DC.

paddock in the grounds, while the Captain and I prepared ourselves – fortunately it was one of the hottest afternoons of a hot summer – by stripping and mounting an unsaddled horse, chosen for the broadness of its back and the placidity of its temper.

We took up first perhaps the easiest posture of those illustrated in the prints: one in which the Captain sat astride the horse in a normal manner, while I sat astride *him*, facing the rear. We trotted slowly round the paddock without the slightest difficulty, but the Comte pointed out amid the applause with which we were greeted that some of the other positions illustrated were not likely to prove so easy. Lifting myself from the Captain's unyielding tool, I next placed myself between his thighs, my knees bent over his elbows as he held the reins, and he inserted his tool by slowly edging himself towards me. This too proved to be a relatively simple matter, though less comfortable and hence less enjoyable than the former.

We halted the horse while we exchanged places, myself lying on its broad back with my head towards the mane, while the Captain supported himself on his knees to mount me as I threw my legs over his shoulders. This was secure enough while the horse stood still, but it was with some difficulty that we maintained our balance while he walked slowly around the paddock. We did, however, complete one circuit, which was enough. The final position, however, defeated us entirely – or, rather, defeated me, for it showed the Mongolian rider standing upon his head, or rather hanging with his head by the horse's neck and his body vertical above him, while the concubine, astride the horse but facing its rear, thrust herself upon him by raising her buttocks and pushing herself backwards with her hands!

Though the Captain maintained both his position and the rigidity of his organ perfectly, I found my part quite impossible to play, and we returned to our first position while he urged the horse to a trot, and allowed himself to reach heaven at last, to the accompaniment of applause from the gathering, whose view it was that we had achieved a display sufficiently accomplished and moving to win at least part of the wager; whereupon the Comte declared, 'not a part, but all', and generously handed me the purse!

I can still, though now many miles from the Château, see in my mind's eye elegant figures moving about those gardens, and in the distance the little white figures of bathers in the still waters of the backwater of the river which curls at the foot of the lawns; there, in a small declivity, was a grotto which became a natural Garden of Eden, in which it was customary to wear no clothes; there the men sunbathed, while the ladies (for whom, to my regret, white skins were as necessary in the bedroom as jewels in the drawing-room) lay in the shade of the trees and bushes; or where dalliance took place, more or less in privacy, sometimes by twos and sometimes by fours or sixes or in odd numbers, while servants in their livery brought refreshing drinks and foods.

I should say that I trained my staff carefully. Both men and women were chosen for their appearance as well as for their accomplishment as servants. They were instructed never to show surprise, whatever they saw or heard, and to be to the last degree discreet. It was always made quite clear to my guests that none of the servants was to be molested, or persuaded for that matter to amorous encounters, unless I had first been informed and had approved. If a maid was fortunate enough to captivate one of the male guests, I had no objection, but then she must decide whether she wished to take her chance; if once she left me, she was not to return, whatever her predicament, and this I made plain. On the other hand, a night's pleasure was nothing I wished to deny to either sex.

The gentlemen who stayed with me often brought their

own mistresses, or counted on my providing one, which indeed was almost invariably the case, my having become acquainted with a number of elegant ladies for whom an illicit pleasure was a strong attraction. As to the men servants, I always encouraged them to enjoy any assignation they cared to make with other members of my staff, and even made it possible for them to maintain their own mistresses among the local village girls. It would have been in the first degree unfair, and even might have led to violence, should a young man find himself spending his whole day in an atmosphere of sensuality – from morning to night attending on couples whose pleasure was in making love – without the means of releasing his own natural feelings. In the course of things, my women guests set their ambitions rather higher than a footman, although it was within my experience that one or two ladies whose aristocratic lovers failed to give entire satisfaction searched for and found robust men whose charms were normally concealed beneath livery.

And so it was that the Château was regarded as a place of the most satisfying and continually relaxed enjoyment, which few approached without anticipation of delight, and from which no-one to my knowledge (save the poor doctor) retired disappointed or in confusion.

CHAPTER FOUR

Liane de Chassigne at her toilet – a select dinner party – an unusual dish – the diners' reactions – Liane a nun – a surprising footman – who further surprises me – and leaves me – the students' ballot – my response – Comte and Vicomte – new lessons in love – and their success – a bride's gratitude – the tributes of wives and other ladies

It was in the autumn of 1864 that I gave my rival Anne de Chassigne, known as Liane, her *congé*. At that time she had reached the heights of her meagre attractions (having wasted herself upon stage-door Johnnies while a dancer at the *Folies*, she was now engaged in dances of a less public but more profitable nature). That gossip M. de Goubouges had delighted in bringing me an acount of how Liane had invited a *côterie* of her most influential admirers to her apartment, and received them sitting in a bath of milk (asses' milk, M. Goubouges opined; cows' milk would have been more fitting). Rising from this bath in a manner most calculated to expose her charms, she had summoned a pair of *filles de ferme* who had dried her with the most lascivious gestures and displays, whereupon she had withdrawn, leaving – or so M. Goubouges reported – her audience in a fever of unassuaged lust. My informant was unnecessarily emphatic about the nature of Liane's charms and the manner in which she exhibited them, and had spread the story all over Paris.

A week later I invited six gentlemen to dinner. The irritating but indispensible M. Goubouges was one, for his tattle I was in need of; then came the Duc de Treage, the Prince C——, Colonel Marc Aubry, M. Paul of the Banque

National, M. Perriport (the brother of the owner of the Restaurant Tric), and the actor Georges Capillon, a friend of Henri Meilhac, Offenbach's librettist, on whom I was eager to make an impression. I let it be known that the chief purpose of the occasion was to display the talents of my chef, Salé, formerly with the Prince d'Orléans, but I hinted to Goubouges that the final dish was likely to be one of an unusual nature.

I received the gentlemen in my finest style, and entertained them to a dinner of excellent quality; the conversation was agreeable, the wines accomplished. When we had finished all but the final course, I excused myself, in order to supervise its presentation. Slipping to the kitchen, I stepped out of my gown (when entertaining gentlemen it is never my habit to wear quantities of underclothing, and especially was this the case on this occasion) and mounting a chair lay upon a vast silver dish which Salé had borrowed for me from the Prince d'Orlèans' kitchen. I lay upon my side, my head upon my hand.

Salé stepped forward, accompanied by Yves, a footman I had employed only recently, carrying as it were his palate (*sic*) – a large tray upon which was a set of dishes filled with marzipans, sauces and pastes, all of different colours. With that deftness and artistry for which he was so famed, Salé began to decorate my naked body with rosettes and swathes of creams and sauces, each carefully composed so that the heat of my body would not melt them before I came to table.

As Salé was laying long trails of cream across my haunches and applying wreaths of tiny button flowers to the upper sides of my breasts, I could not help noticing that Yves, chosen like all my servants for a combination of personal charm and accomplishment, and a young man of obvious and ever-increasingly virile promise, was taking a peculiar interest in the chef's work. The knuckles of his hands were whiter than would have been the case had the tray been ten times as heavy, and the state of his breeches proclaimed the fact that his attitude to his employer was one of greater warmth than respect.

Having finished the decoration by placing a single un-peeled grape in the dint of my navel, Salé piled innumerable *meringues* about the dish, completing the effect with a dusting of icing sugar. The vast cover which belonged to the dish was then placed over me, and I heard Salé call the other two footmen into the room. Shortly afterwards I felt myself being raised, and carried down the passage to the dining-room. I heard the door opened, and the chatter of voices cease as the dish was carried in and settled upon the table.[1]

When the lid was lifted, I was rewarded by finding myself the centre of a ring of round eyes and half-open mouths. M. Paul, as I had expected, was the first to recover, and with an affectation of coolness reached out, removed the grape, and slipped it slowly between his lips. Not to be outdone, M. Perriport leant forward and applied his tongue to removing the small white flower that Salé had placed upon my right tit; and then all, except for M. Goubouges, who as I expected was as usual content simply to observe and record, were at me, kneeling upon their chairs or upon the table, their fingers and tongues busy at every part of me as they lifted and licked the sweetness from my body. The Prince was so inflamed by the circumstances that nothing would content him other than to have me there and then upon the table, to the ruination of the remaining decora-tion upon my body, and the irritation of the other gentle-men, in whom only reverence for rank restricted violence.

So speedily did the Prince fetch off that they had not to

[1] Previous accounts of Cora Pearl's life have recorded that she was served up naked on a silver dish at the Café Anglais, an event unmentioned in this text.

wait long – *le laurier est tot coupé*, as my friend Théo used to say.[2] Since the centre of a dining-table and a mess of *meringues* together with wine-glasses and forks is not the most convenient nor comfortable of pleasure-beds, the price of my comforting the other members of the party was that they should give me time at least to dispose myself on one of the nearby couches, where the Duc continued where the Prince had left off; M. Capillon as was his wont contented himself with an energetic frigging (often the taste of members of his profession, I have frequently been disappointed to observe), while M. Paul offered his shaft to my lips and Colonel Aubry his to my sufficiently practised manual manipulation. Finally, M. Perriport, in a desperate fit of agitation, was attempting to displace the Duc when his ecstacy overflowed, together with an excess of language which seemed to me to betray a youth spent in less than polite circles.

The way in which (to offer an observation often made by me) gentlemen, whether they are intimates or no, are perfectly agreeable to make love to the same woman at the same time, is strange. It may be a circumstance of nature that one woman may in a trice satisfy six or seven men or even more, while it is impossible for the most virile of fellows to satisfy more than three women in twenty minutes or so; but that men should positively seek such a *commission* of fellow lovers when they would hesitate to bathe themselves in the same water or put on each other's pantaloons, is surprising to me. However, such is very often the case, as it seems that the butting of one pair of buttocks may quicken the butting of another. And often, as in this case, the result is a remarkably speedy accomplishment of all desires. My friends took their leave kindly,

[2] The quotation is of course from Théodore de Banville's *Les Cariatides*, somewhat mangled. There is no indication that de Banville was a lover of Cora Pearl, though it is possible.

leaving me entirely satisfied that M. Goubouges' account of the occasion would entirely eclipse the memory of Liane's batheing party; as indeed by noon of the next day proved to be the case. Shortly afterwards she became a postulant nun, under the name of Soeur Madeleine de la Penitence.

I was not tired but elated by my triumph; and the rapid accomplishment of both the Prince's and the Duc's desires left me at a pitch of irritation. So upon retiring to my bedroom to bath, I ordered that Yves should bring me my hot water, and when he did so ordered him to assist me. Up to that time I had always embraced the admirable French motto, *jamais avec les domestiques*;[3] but my observation of the boy's passion for me had roused me to try him. As he gave me his hand to help me step into the bath, I told him to remove his livery, for, said I, it had cost several hundred francs, and I was not eager it should be soiled.

To my surprise, he not only threw it off with remarkable celerity, but his underclothes with it. (It has been my general observation that members of the lower order, while as lusty as any gentleman, tend to satisfy themselves while removing as little clothing as is convenient for the purpose of the Act.) He then washed me all over with his hands, which were both clean and gentle, his manhood meanwhile paying me the compliment of raising, nodding and weeping at my beauties.

The sight of his marvellously promising person moved me to allow him to draw me from my bath and to the rugs beside the bed, where he dried me with his own body, proving that as I had suspected a footman was capable of much more stamina than any man of society. At least, that was what I believed him to prove; though even in the ecstacy to which his ministerings of hand, tongue and

[3] 'Never with the servants'; the better-known phrase, employed in English bourgeois homes when the conversation became intimate, was 'Not *before* the servants'.

manhood thrice roused me, I retained the power to wonder at the extent of his understanding of the requirements of my sex. Unlike most men of whatever rank, he did not batter at my gate until his ram broke, but as in a mirror seemed to attack me with my own weapons; how good a whore he would have made was what occurred to me, had it been the custom for men to enter our profession. The graceful, almost womanly but yet wholly masculine manner in which he seemed to subdue his own pleasure to mine (a quality rarely found) amazed me. It was some time before we were spent; and when at last it was so, I taxed him with being no servant. Nor was he.

I cannot even yet reveal his family name, for it was one with the most formidable respectable history, not unconnected with Holy Church; Yves (it is not his proper name) was a young Vicomte who had loved me passionately at a distance for over three years, and later revealed to me that he had been the author of a love-sick letter written to me when he was a mere schoolboy, to whose unformed note I had sent a cool, if not unkind, reply. He repaid me now by serving me in the most menial way for some weeks, trusting that an opportunity would arise for him to declare himself, which he now did – and continued to do for some weeks when, relieving him of his menial duty, I relieved him also of his livery, maintaining him in my bedroom as a body servant whose duty was entirely to minister to my pleasure. He, far from objecting to this, seemed to welcome it.

Yves was my lover for several weeks – until one day when I had expressed the intention to go for the day to a friend in Clichy, returning only late in the evening. Unfortunately, or perhaps fortunately, my friend was away, and I returned to the Rue de Chaillot several hours before I was expected. Entering the house, I went upstairs to my rooms without even pausing to take off my topcoat; imagine my surprise when, opening the door of my bedroom, I saw two naked figures upon the bed! Yves was lying upon his back with his head at the bottom of the bed, while over him crouched, on all fours, the figure of a pretty boyish girl whose lips were ministering to him while he, his head lifted, was lavishing kisses between her thighs. Hearing my gasp of surprising and, I must confess, fury – I was not used to my lovers entertaining others in my very bed, whatever they might do when away from me – Yves' head fell back and his astonished eyes met mine; but mine were irresistibly drawn elsewhere, for as his head revealed the full quarters of his lover, I saw not the mossy mount of a girl, but the pendant stones and tool of a boy, and as the latter jumped away and sat up, I saw the pug-face of a street-urchin.

I strode forward and administered a sharp slap to the still pulsing tool of the lad, who gave a yowl of pain and scampered for his filthy clothes which lay by the bed. Yves, however, remained lying on the bed with the utmost *sang-froid*, and after he had thrown a coin to the lad, who snatched it up and made out of the door and away, was sufficiently impertinent to reach for my hand and attempt to draw me towards the bed to enable me to continue in satisfying him! I had at that time still, however, a mistrust of gentlemen whose satisfaction could be even partially found with members of their own sex, and took the haughty stand; whereupon Yves with the greatest coolness requested me to send for his clothes, maintaining he would leave me.

It was to my own surprise that, seeing him sitting there, his strong and manly chest tapering to a girlish waist, below which his great instrument was only beginning to dissipate itself among the mass of gold curls which lay around it, I found myself stirred, and forced to make friends anew; and within moments he was indeed thrusting into my happy parts the weapon honed for me by the mouth of the street lad! As we lay quiet after his rapture and my own, Yves explained that during his years in a military academy he had become used to the taste of boys' flesh, and that while he found me a lavish tonic for his senses, during my absence he had suddenly found himself longing for (as he put it) a taste of lad, and seeing the boy from the window, had summoned him. He could rarely, he said, make love exclusively to women for more than a week or two, although he had never found himself so loving a male as to wish to belong exclusively to him.

The boy, for whom the experience had plainly not been an exclusive one, had soon struck the bargain and found his way to my room by the simple device of a down-pipe. There, Yves had at first thrown the boy's legs over his shoulders and attempted to apply himself to the only aperture with which the Creator had provided him; but his instrument proved too large, and anxious not to hurt the lad – for Yves was above all of a considerate nature – he had instead, after washing him thoroughly (with, I may say, my own sponges and soaps!) taken recourse to the enjoyment which I had interrupted, and had been on the point of giving up his soul between the boys' practised lips, when I had come in. Knowing the pleasure my own lips took in receiving between them the soft and smooth, hard and slippery tool of a lover, I could not but sympathize with one from whom convention sought to remove the pleasure, and in short no breach was driven between Yves and myself on this occasion, though in the course of not too long a time he left me.

In the profession to which I have the honour to belong, it is necessarily an obligation to make oneself agreeable to gentlemen of all constitutions, and I count it my good fortune that while I have been attractive to men who, while of high place and often of high wealth, have not necessarily possessed great beauty of body or nature, I have also attracted the admiration of the young – of those perhaps below my own years so much as to be almost children.

It was in 1864, if I remember aright, that I was alone in the house one evening when there was a peremptory ringing at the bell. My girl told me that a young man had presented himself, and insisted on seeing me. I had him shown up, on the assurance that he appeared respectable, and in came a boy of perhaps seventeen, in a velvet coat and with a nervous look about him. He appeared incapable of expressing what he desired, but upon being placed in a chair and fortified with wine, produced a purse of fifty louis and laid it on the table. Though not specially in a mood for dalliance, I found the look he directed upon me when, leading him into the next room, I divested myself of my clothes, a positive aphrodisiac, and was able to answer his ardour with my own for the relatively brief period during which he was able to retain his advantage.

As he lay with his head upon my arm, I asked how he had come to visit me, and he revealed that he was one of a group of fifty students who had been used to admiring me as I passed to and fro from my house, or at the opera, where with glasses they observed me in my box. Since they were poor, it was clear that none of them would ever taste my favours; but driven by the ingeniousness of youth, and the taste of the time for communal action, they contributed one louis each to the purse, and had drawn lots for the pleasure. My lover had won.

This tribute won my heart completely; so that not only did I respond to the student's renewed ardour as fully as he might wish (the five minutes' gratification which he had previously derived before his death having been in my view scant value), but took one louis from the purse and returned it to him, saying that I had enjoyed his company and commended his spirit, and was happy that he should have me without the necessity of payment.

It was during this period too that I had the pleasure of

satisfying the desires both of Comte Napoléon Daru and of his son the Vicomte Paul, one a fine and active man of perhaps forty-eight years, and the other a boy of nineteen. They did not of course attend me on the same night, but often on following nights, and it was with interest that I noticed the difference between them, which was not one of years – for the Vicomte was in fact the less ardent of the two, while his father retained the agility and ardour of a man half his age – but of temperament: the Comte was as full of tricks as a monkey, and as inventive, so that even when I was least in the mood for amorous play, he could rouse me to a delightful pitch; while his son, the Vicomte, was of a phlegmatic disposition, disinclined for anything but the quickest congress, lying on top of me and declining to participate in the slightest deviation from that single position.

Though the gifts with which the Vicomte showered me were generous enough (I suspect that he was encouraged in this by his father, for I do not believe it was in his own nature), I have never been one to be satisfied by a mere cipher in lovemaking, and determined to teach the youth better manners. Waiting until an evening when he showed at least the shadow of an interest in having me, I declined to let him at me until he would agree to taking me as I sat on the edge of my dressing table. This, as those who have tried it will confirm, enables one a freedom of action which is impossible in a reclining position, and I was able to caress his buttocks and the small of his back, to tumble his stones and to tickle with my fingers the sensitive spot between them and the fundament. His surprise was palpable, but his enjoyment no less so, and having discovered that (as he put it) there were more ways than one of cracking an egg, he soon became no less inventive than myself, seducing me into play upon the rugs of the floor, before a combination of mirrors, between the courses at the dinner-table, and even upon one occasion on the stairs from the hallway to the dining-room, where we almost upset the footman carrying up the first course, which, having been carefully trained to ignore anything but his duty, he nevertheless successfully conducted to-the table, where no more than somewhat breathless, we enjoyed it.

Whether or not his father, the Comte, was aware of my schooling I do not know, but it was he who announced to me shortly afterwards that he had betrothed his son to a young heiress of my acquaintance. The news interested me strongly, for I had taken the precaution of obtaining the Vicomte's name on a written guarantee to pay me two hundred thousand francs on the occasion of his marriage. (I remember the occasion of its signing perfectly well; young Daru wished me to allow him to cover my body with a nauseous black treacle to which he was addicted, so that he could lick it from me; and the damage to my sheets and the discomfort to me encouraged me to put that price upon it, which he happily consented to.)

The marriage duly took place, but upon my writing to the Vicomte to ask for my dowry, I received no acknowledgement. After writing to him on more than three occasions with no response, I reluctantly sent the document with his signature upon it to the new Vicomtesse. Within two days, to my great surprise, the lady called upon me – a girl a year or two younger than myself, of considerable beauty. I was amazed when she addressed me with affection rather than *politesse*, and handed over the money in gold upon the spot. More than that, she thanked me for my 'generosity'. When I repeated the word, enquiringly, that delightful creature actually blushed – whereupon I took it to be the case that she was in no doubt to whom she owed the Vicomte's expertise in the bedroom, which she presently enjoyed. We parted good friends.

It will perhaps be taken as remarkable by the reader who

has had no experience of these matters, that I was the subject of virtually no jealousy from the wives of those men who paid me tribute. It may be that they were all conscious of the extent to which I educated their husbands, for however polite the wife may be at the dinner table or in the salon, there is little doubt that her appetite is less carefully restrained in the bedroom, and the man who cannot there cook up a dish to her satisfaction is to be pitied. It may be that a few ladies were grateful to me for satisfying appetites too ardent for them, or appetites they for some reason did not wish to cater to; but they were well in a minority, and most of them of a lesbian disposition. The first time one of these ladies invited me to display my breasts to her, I was surprised, though my doing so involved me in no intimacy with her. On other occasions I had to repel the advances of certain ladies, who came to me in private hoping to purchase those favours I sold their husbands. I have never since my school days been especially attracted to other women for the purpose of the act of love with them (if so it can be called). I have no objection to it; but unlike most of my amorous combats, it has been a matter of business rather than pleasure when I have consented – except on one occasion, which I will relate in its place.

CHAPTER FIVE

*Friends, and others – Caro Letessier – the Russian in love –
La Barucci – ah! que j'aime les militaires – the Prince of
Wales amused – Caro Hassé at Oxford – Dr Bulley charmed
– Mr Longfellow's tribute – Adèle Courtois – La Paiva –
Herr Wagner – the False Emperor – the bouchons de carafe –
a canine betrayal – beauty enhanced – death of Morny – the
Duc de Caderousse – his excesses – Des Varennes – bathed in
brandy – make up – my influence on fashion – Prince
Napoléon – his mistresses – his wife – a less than ardent lover
– his generosity – the Rue de Chaillot – Brunet and Hurion –
the vital parts of men; various – mutual pleasures*

I have often heard it said that the years before the Siege
were the greatest years of Paris society; certainly this was
the case for me. Things were never quite the same afterwards. And it was true for at least some of my friends, who
followed the same profession as myself. I say 'friends', but
of course in our profession as in others, the word can have
various degrees of meaning. Some of my sisters were indeed
friends – and I must pay tribute to Caroline Letessier, who
was to give me shelter when the world turned against me.

Caro perhaps lacks the *hauteur* which makes for the very
highest society among us; but her good nature, shown in
her pretty little round face with its impudent grin, is
transparent. She has always kept her early life dark, though
she did tell me once that she knew neither of her parents,
and that her earliest memory was of living with a butcher
called Graindorge in a poor quarter of Paris. From the

earliest years she shared his bed, and after his wife died, looked after the poor single room which they inhabited. The butcher introduced her to the pleasures of love at a very early age, though, she assured me, without any insistence or pain to her; they began with a mutual toying and a natural desire for human comfort, and grew to taking their full pleasure as soon as Caro was big enough, about her fourteenth year. Soon afterwards, however, the butcher married again – to the widow of a wine merchant, who did not care for a foster-daughter as pretty as she; and so Caro found herself thrown upon the streets.

Her next years were no doubt as bad as can be imagined; she would never speak of them. But within three years she had found her way to Turin, where she was a dancer at the French Theatre. She was in those days remarkably slim – in fact, thin would be more the word if her description is accurate; 'just like a boy', she used to tell me, and indeed her first protector, a French diplomat, had been inclined to the company of boys, and could only make love to girls who resembled them. His wife threatened to leave him if he continued to indulge his former taste, and he was delighted with Caro because she could provoke him to venery, especially if she presented him with a view of her tight little arse. So he was able to gain the reputation of a ladies' man, which formerly he had signally lacked, and satisfy his wife's vanity.

Within a short time, Caro was the toast of Turin, and when she returned to Paris it was with introductions to the very highest society. We met first in 1859, when I was still almost unknown, at the Théâtre du Palais-Royal, where she was a dancer. At one time I thought of finding employment there, and had been turned disappointed from the stage door when Caro came out, grinned at me with a very welcome friendliness, and took me back for a drink at her house – wonderfully furnished, and in the utmost of style and luxury. She gave me much good advice, and I thought I had found a friend. She showed me around her rooms, including the bedroom with its gold-framed mirrors all around the huge bed, beside which on a table stood the golden apple in which she kept her rice-powder. In a cupboard nearby were a variety of costumes in which she entertained some of her lovers, including a large cloak of fur lined with black silk, and a peasant's shirt and trousers (which, she told me, she had to put on when a certain prince came to see her, smearing her face with dirt and her body with excrement).

Our friendship then was of brief duration, for within a month she had left Paris for St Petersburg, where she appeared at the Théâtre Michel and became the mistress of a Grand Duke (who, when the top half of her dress was torn from her shoulders one evening at a ball, threaded the ribbon of the Grand Cordon of the Order of St Andrew through the tattered remains, to support them about her body). She and the Grand Duke eloped together from Petersburg in 1867, but at Berlin Russian agents caught up with them, and the Duke (the nephew of the Tsar) was ordered to return to Russia. He refused, and they settled down as M. and Mme Letessier at Baden, where they were welcomed in society by everybody except the notorious actress Hortense Schneider, who meeting Caro at the casino one evening remarked loudly to her companion, 'I have seen many a fatted calf, but never one so pretty.' At which Caro as loudly remarked to the Duke that she had never seen such a fat cow. The riposte, while frank enough, was unfortunately insufficiently witty to pass muster, and almost resulted in Caro being thrown out of Baden; fortunately, however, years previously she had been engaged by the Grand Duchess there to educate her son in those matters she was best qualified to teach, and she intervened.

Not long afterwards, however, Caro returned to Paris alone, and it was then that we really became friends; she was endlessly entertaining, with her constant tales of the behaviour of the mad Russians, as she called them, whose main idea seemed to be always to combine love-making with getting drunk. Caro maintains that the Russian is the only man who can be drunk almost to the point of collapse without losing the power to please a woman; in fact, she always insists that there came a point at which a Russian's tool, once engorged, resisted all attempts to satiate it, so that however many times he was brought to the point, it was still possible for him to continue to satisfy another mistress – even if he was unconscious with schnapps. I find this difficult to believe, for I have always found alcohol, in men, an enemy to persistence.

Caro was always extremely popular with foreigners; Frenchmen, I believe, mostly found her too thin, but English, Germans, Russians thought her to be a typical Parisienne, with her jet black hair, her gaiety and her slim figure (though after her return from Baden she had put on a little weight, so that her breasts became a feature of her beauty rather than a mere accompaniment to it). The whiteness of her body was also an attraction; like most Parisiennes, she refused to expose herself to the sun, with the result that her body was always as white as paper. Recently, now we are much together, I came unexpectely into her room to find her lying beneath the body of a man who I took to be an Indian. Later, he was introduced to me as a Lieutenant in the British Navy (though an aristocrat); my mistake had been the result of seeing her white limbs next to those of a man who had spent many hours almost naked upon the deck of a ship.

If Caro and I were at the opposite poles of taste where the gentlemen were concerned, she the true Parisienne, I the Englishwoman, La Barucci came somewhere between us. I was never so friendly with Giulia Beneni as with Caro, partly because I have never cared for Italian women with their continual obsession with babies. But certainly La Barucci, as she became known, was less objectionable than some of the Mamas I have known. She had been born in Rome in the same year as myself, though I am told she looks older, and came to Paris when she was a very young girl as the mistress of a M. de Danne. He made the mistake of taking her to the Café de Rondale, where she stared into the large mirror which stood at the end of the salon, and exclaimed loudly and in very bad French, '*Grande Dio! mais je suis belle!*'

The Prince d'Hénin, dining there that same evening, agreed with her, and stole her immediately from poor M. de Danne, installing her in rooms on the Champs Élysées, where within a month she had accumulated a collection of jewellery said to be worth a million francs. She did this by the very simple means of never saying no to any man who approached her, and readily satisfying him in whatever manner he required, however vulgar. She was besotted by money, but also, to be fair to her, by soldiers; even if she had just entertained a member of the Jockey Club and was exhausted by excess, seeing a good tall fellow in uniform she would immediately dress and follow him, not taking no for an answer. On one occasion she followed to his barracks the captain commanding the Tuilerie detachment, and made her way into the room which he occupied on night duty. When his sergeant entered to report at midnight, he found his commanding officer clad only in his shirt, beneath the tails of which La Barucci was at work with her lips (she had, especially with soldiers, a great love of applying herself in this way to a man's tool, to which taste Italian women, I have often remarked, are peculiarly devoted). The sergeant reported the incident, but the Emperor was more amused than angry, and the captain escaped rebuke. He was, however, pilloried in the press, and later by M. Offenbach, whose number in *La Grande-Duchesse de Gérolstein,* '*Ah! que j'aime les militaires!*' was based on the incident.

La Barucci's rooms at 124, Avenue des Champs-Élysées made her an income in more ways than one, for she was happy to let them out to married women who wished for somewhere to entertain their lovers; and it is said that she also received money on occasion for allowing other clients to occupy the neighbouring room, from which, through an aperture in the wall, they could watch the entertainment unknowingly provided by a couple in mutual ecstasy. This source of income ceased, however, when a member of the Government whose passion for *voyeurism* proved to be satisfied by the sight of one of his colleagues making love to his wife forced La Barucci to stop up the hole in the wall.

For a while, La Barucci was excessively successful – more so than either Caro or myself; members of the Imperial Family called upon her, and Parisian society gambled at her rooms, and was entertained to great dinners and a variety of other amusements. She had the utmost daring. It was said that when the Prince of Wales visited Paris, and she was invited to the Maison d'Or to meet him, she arrived forty-five minutes late, and when the Duc de Grammont-Caderousse presented her, lifted her hands to her shoulders, releasing her gown, which dropped to the floor revealing her quite naked except for fifteen strings of pearls. Later, when the Duc remonstrated, she replied: 'I showed him the finest property I own, and I make no charge!'

La Barucci's pearls were famous; they were supposed to be worth two hundred thousand francs. It is said that once, when she fell violently in love with a student and brought him back to her rooms, the sight of the pearls so unmanned him that despite her very best endeavours he was unable to pay her the tribute she expected. But it may be that when he saw her unclothed, she was less attractive than in her finery, for she lost her figure early in her career; and while in her fine clothes and jewels she still looked beautiful, her sagging breasts and pot-belly defied even the light of the single candle which stood at her bedside, and men who had been crazy to become her lovers never visited her again, once having seen her naked, despite all her lascivious tricks.

In general, I got on well both with Caro and with La Barucci, but my relations with other colleagues were not always easy, due to their frequent jealousy. Though I shared apartments for a time with Caroline Hassé, as I have recorded, she was too vulgar to retain my respect. With her large frame she looked more like Louis-Phillipe than anyone else, and I was surprised that for a while she became the close friend of *my* Caro, Letessier. In fact during the siege of Paris in 1870 they went together to England, where they visited an undergraduate at Magdalen College, Oxford (who had got to know them in Paris, where his parents lived). The two Carolines were set up in rooms at the Randolph Hotel, and one of the dons of Magdalen fell violently in love with my Caro, who used to visit him in his rooms, where he rogered her enthusiastically while undergraduates were waiting next door for their lessons. One of the Fellows[1] suspected the morals of the young visitor, and after a while reported the circumstances to the President of the College, Dr Bulley, who was introduced to both women at the Botanical Gardens, where they charmed him to the extent that he presented them to Oxford society as 'refugees from the besieged French capital'. Among the men who met them was a visiting American poet, Mr Longfellow, who is said to have written some highly

[1] Charles Reade, 1814–84, author of *The Cloister and the Hearth*. While at Oxford Caroline visited Christ Church College, and played croquet with the daughters of the Dean – one of whom was the original Alice of 'Lewis Caroll's' book.

indecent verses celebrating Caroline Hassé. The undergraduate who had brought them there is now a prominent
man in Oxford, much involved with church affairs.

It was Caro Hassé who, soon after we parted, painted her
barouche yellow, to spite the Princess von Metternich, the
wife of the Austrian Ambassador (Barucci's was blue and
red, my own blue). She eventually set her rooms in the Rue
de Pontheiu on fire as a result of too great an eagerness to
illuminate the figures of a negro and two street whores she
had engaged to entertain the Comte de Maugny.

Adèle Courtois, who called herself the Baronne de
Sternberg, was a woman I never greatly cared for. Very
early in her career she avoided the necessity to earn her
bread by contriving an alliance or morganatic marriage with
the Baron, who allowed her ten thousand francs a month,
and since he was an elderly man while she was young, gave
her permission to keep a young lover; had the Baron kept a
closer watch on her, he would have perceived that the face
of that young lover changed remarkably from month to
month, at one time resembling that of a stable-boy, at
another that of a footman, yet again that of a fellow from a
nearby bakery. However, the Baron was complaisant, and
the Baronne happy.

It has been said by those who know nothing about it,
that I had a bitter quarrel with La Paiva. While certainly
that woman always seemed to me to be lacking in any kind
of virtue, I would never have lowered myself to quarrel
with her in public, much less to horse-whip her in the Bois,
as has been suggested. If I had, she would not have
survived, for she was by no means robust (one heard that
she was born of a union between a witch and her broom-
stick-handle). She was a Russian who came to Paris in 1836,
and astonishingly made her way very quickly into society –
not, goodness knows, because of her looks; bony and thin,
she had goggle-eyes and a big nose as well as a protruding

chin. However, what she lacked in beauty she made up for in spirit, and could not only perform the act of love for seven or eight hours with an equal number of men without apparent fatigue, but was said to be able by her lascivious ways (which included a mastery of obscene words and phrases in most European languages) to raise a man from the dead quicker than any other woman in Paris.

She once married Henri Herz, the piano-maker, and a very rich man, but was refused entry to the Court when Herz tried to present her there, and instead created a salon of her own attended by many musicians including the German composer Wagner (whose cheap violet scent, she said, almost made her vomit). While Herz was out of the country, his family, outraged by La Paiva's expenditure of his fortune, threw her out of the house, and after going to London for a few months, where she was the mistress of Lord Stanley, she 'married' a Portuguese marquis, Albino-Francesco de Paiva-Araujo. It was always said that on the morning after the wedding she congratulated him on achieving his ambition, to sleep with her, and announced her intention of using his title to make herself the best-known whore in Europe. He shot himself some years later. She returned to Paris, and there captivated the Count Guido Henckel von Donnermarck, eleven years her junior and not nearly her equal in experience.

In her mansion in the Place St-George, she entertained magnificently, and – now that she had a fortune – without regard to money. When Adolph Gaiffe, a young man without a fortune, sought her favours, she told him she would charge him ten thousand francs – but not in the normal way. He should set fire to the notes, and as long as they burned, he could make love to her. He brought the money, spread it out as economically as possible, set fire to the first note (having first divested himself of his clothing) and threw himself on La Paiva, managing to reach his crisis before the last note was extinguished. He then revealed that they had all been forgeries.

All Paris was amused; but all Paris was always amused by her excesses, for only the men besotted by her erotic nature saw anything attractive about her. The rest saw only an ambitious fool, sneered at her extravagance, condemned her vulgarity. One evening she was highly delighted when the Emperor himself was announced during dinner at her house. When he entered and sat himself next to her, announcing the award of decorations to all her guests, and in other ways made himself agreeable, she felt she had reached the peak of social ambition. She was, it was true, slightly surprised when without further ado His Majesty thrust his hand into her bosom, drawing a breast from her dress to fasten his lips on it. Her surprise changed to horror when his little beard became entangled in one of the jewels of her corsage. When he straightened up, however, the beard remained, and he was revealed as the clean-shaven Vivier, the horn-player, who looked remarkably like the Emperor.

La Paiva's house (designed for her by Pierre Mauguin, and taking ten years to build) and her Château at Pont-chartain (which cost von Donnersmarck two million francs) were decorated with a luxury which few other women of the age could have afforded, and she never ventured into public without being covered from head to foot with jewels, including two diamonds so big that they were spoken of as *bouchons de carafe*.[2] Yet she never succeeded in making her way, in becoming a real leader of society; and those who attended her so-called salon did so only to be able to look about them and sneer at her afterwards. It is beyond me how she managed to amass such a fortune; she always spoke of success as something which could be

---

[2] glass-stoppers.

achieved by willpower alone, and since one really could not imagine that any man would want to sleep with her at the sight of her ill-favoured face and more ill-favoured body, I imagine that indeed sheer willpower (or some witchcraft inherited from her mother) was the reason.

It was not only of those of us whose lives were given up entirely to pleasure that scandalous anecdotes were told; the romances of those higher in polite society gave rise to amusing incidents. For instance, the Princess Mathilde had a long-term alliance with the spectacularly handsome Comte de Nieuwekerke – so long that it was virtually a marriage. One day when the Princess was entertaining to tea some of the women whose attitude is that nothing improper can be admitted to attach itself to their friends, the door was pushed open by her delightful little miniature greyhound dog, which leaped on to the Princess' lap. She immediately pushed it off, saying 'Get down, you bad dog; you know you are in disgrace!' When the ladies enquired the reason, the Princess explained that all the previous night the dog had kept climbing on to her bed, and had kept her awake.

Just then, Nieuwekerke was announced, and greeted the Princess with the same polite deference as the other ladies. The Princess told him how happy she was to see him after so long an absence, when the little dog jumped up to greet him. He immediately pushed it away, and thoughtlessly rebuked it: 'No, no, get down, you bad dog; you forget you did not allow me to sleep a wink last night jumping on my bed so often!'

I spent a great deal of money on my own living quarters at Beauséjour. The château had, for instance, a large bronze bath which was cast for me by Chevalier of Paris, with my monogram engraved upon it, and there was plenty of marble and brasswork about the place, and even some gold! But my main extravagance was cleanliness: my floors were polished sometimes several times a day, and a team of servants was engaged to that end. In the Paris house, things sparkled equally brightly; the bathroom there was of rose marble, and my initials were placed in gold at the bottom of the bath, where they were polished daily, and sometimes twice daily, by material soft as any lawn.

I always looked upon the furnishings of any place in which I lived as a setting for my person, and everthing was planned to enhance my attractions. This may sound vain; in fact, it is good business, and a means of insurance. After seventeen, none of us grow more beautiful in body, though we may be more seductive in other ways. We need the flattery of silks and satins, of candles in silver sconces, of mirrors with gold about them, so that our lovers, once enticed by our personality, may believe us as beautiful as they have painted us in their mind's eye. I have seen many a man, while I have toyed with him, admiring in the mirror the candle-lit reflection of our naked bodies, and by placing myself so that his body has been between mine and the glass (for most men love watching themselves at work) I have emphasized my own beauty. By the time the lover is ready to turn his attention from the picture to the reality, hands and tongue have done their work, and his ecstacy is such that his only wish is for an activity which makes perfection of form a secondary consideration. This is something which most professional women understand, but which the amateur is deficient in, and something which might profitably be learned by every girl at school.

The death, of my good friend Morny in March 1865 deprived me of more than a lover. He had continued my education in the arts – spending many evenings playing the pianoforte to me, the picture of romance in his velvet smoking jacket; he never desired to keep me entirely to himself, and was even amused to hear my stories of other lovers, while I naturally declined to reveal to him their names. I remember well how he laughed when I told him of the message sent by a well-known lady whose identity I had better conceal, when she was approached by a hopeful lover:

I am at home between twelve and two when the sun shines; all day when it is wet; all evening when a man woos me, and all night when he loves me!

Morny remained so *soigné* to the last that he even forced his wife to attend a ball when he was positively on his death bed; and while he was ordering his servants to put his papers in order and bidding his friends farewell. His father, once the Queen's lover, the Comte de Flahaut, came to sit by his son's bedside, holding his hand; a fine old man, though I was never introduced to him. The Emperor came too, to say his farewell, and was seen leaving Morny's room in tears not only for a brother but for an adviser and astute politician.

The funeral was at the Madeleine, and was crowded; I followed afterwards to the Père Lachaise, together with many others, including soldiers and politicians and at least six of his other mistresses.

Ten days after Morny's death, the Duc de Gramont-Caderousse[3] called on me to express his condolences. Gramont-Caderousse had for some time been the lover of Hortense Schneider, an actress who created the famous role of Mimi in *Les Mémoires de Mini Bamboche* at the Théâtre du Palais-Royal, but whose private life was so enthusiastically amorous that some wit called her '*le passage des princes*'. I doubt very much whether she was aware of Gramont-Caderousse's intention to express his sympathy with me; a sympathy which prompted him to embrace me violently the moment my footman had left us, thrusting his hand into my bosom, and fixing his lips to my breast before

[3] 1835–65

clutching me to him, falling to the floor, thrusting up my skirts, opening his trousers and taking me there and then without further ceremony. The love-making of this admired man was always brusque, and far from the mirror of his public behaviour, for he always claimed to see women as the exemplars of modesty and innocence. It was he, after all, who had fought a duel with a man who had blasphemed against the Virgin Mary, not because he was at all religious, but because he 'could not bear to hear anything ill said of a lady'! He even defended women under what for others would have been embarrassing circumstances. At a time when he was making love to the wife of the Duc de Persigny, unknown to that gentleman, Persigny was heard to complain of his unhappiness at home. Instantly, Gramont-Caderousse replied: 'I cannot permit your grace to say anything against my mistress!'

At the time I knew him, he was thirty years of age, yet looked much older; I am told that his dissipation was exceeded by no-one, although I must admit that he never attempted to involve me in anything more than a quick tumble between the sheets, or for the most part upon the floor. In September of 1865 he died, it was said of consumption, but in my belief of his excesses. I was not invited to his famous last party when, having received the consolation of the church, he gave his friends a first-rate supper, attended by a large number of very young whores, and peacefully died while they were enjoying themselves in the neighbouring room. In many ways he was a most accommodating, considerate man.

It was, in the vulgar, business as usual for a while after Morny's death. I continued to receive the attentions of various gentlemen, and for a while my only regular lover was a rich naval lieutenant, Des Varannes. He had called upon me one afternoon, on the recommendation of a friend, and presented me with a small but beautiful and very heavy vase, which however elegant seemed to me not to be the sort of present which a young man might bring who was expecting more than a glass of tea. After I had examined it, Des Varannes took it from me and asked my permission to place it upon a shelf nearby. But instead of doing so, he deliberately hurled it into the fire place, where it shattered, covering the hearth with gold coins! This act was typical of Des Varannes, for whom nothing was quite as straightforward as it seemed. He would for instance insist on dressing in some of my clothing, while I had to climb into his tight naval uniform, when he would immediately be consumed with passion, and once absolutely ripped his trousers from me with such force that they came into two, and he had to send to his rooms for more.

He was much addicted to brandy, though not to an uncomfortable excess; he would always have a flask of it nearby, however, and would often bathe my limbs in the liquid, lapping it from my body with every appearance of pleasure, and leaving behind a cool and stimulating thrill upon my skin. He was an uncommonly hairy man, and as I stroked his back and buttocks it was as though I was lying with a leopard or a lion, so close lay the hair upon him; as we grew heated, indeed, the sensation was quite uncomfortable, for the perspiration made his hide (I can call it nothing else) knit into little spikes which pricked my breasts and belly.

I think it was at about this time, or perhaps a little earlier, that I brought to Paris the habit of making up. Some of the ladies of the theatre had the habit of retaining their stage make up during the late evening, but with ludicrous results, for their faces appeared pink or orange, unlike anything human. I had the idea that it should be possible to apply a lighter paint which would enhance the visage without making it ridiculous, and experimented at first alone, painting my face with tints of various colours, even including silver and pearl; I also used a dye from London to make my red hair yellow. When I first ventured forth after such an experiment, I was much admired; and soon I had requests from other ladies to show them the art, which I was pleased to do, and for several years would throw open my rooms, where both ladies and gentlemen would come to see me make up.

I was at the height of beauty, and it is only fair to admit that I looked upon those occasions as times of advertisement. I would commonly wear only a dressing-gown, and when I came to make up my neck and bosom, would throw if from my shoulders, so that the ladies and gentlemen could see my figure as I turned to right and to left (it is a scene that M. Zola the novelist was later to use in his novel *Nana*,[4] though he hesitated to report it truly, as only the woman's lover was present in the novel). Few of the gentlemen made their approaches to me; many of them were themselves interested in the art of painting, for they were sodomites, and wished to use it for their own courses. But I have no doubt that the ladies spread the news of my attractions, for strangely some women like to boast of others' beauties while displaying their own.

It seems to me that no writers on fashion take account of the contribution I and my colleagues in the art of love have made to the development of fashion. It is surely true, for instance, that we brought a new gaiety, life and colour to styles which otherwise would have remained of a dullness to stagger reason! Bright colours, a masculine style of attire, men's *paletots*,[5] men's collars, cravats and walking-sticks were never my style, but some of my friends adopted them with great success, and they had their effect on

[4] but the original of Nana was always understood to be another courtesan, Blanche d'Antigny, who bought Cora Pearl's house in the Rue de Chaillot from her.
[5] greatcoats.

women's fashions with their military coats of yellow velvet, with Chinese embroidery, red velvet mantles trimmed with black lace, black *tulle* dresses with gold lace. One particular friend brought in the Diana bodice, leaving one shoulder uncovered, and I myself can claim to have had some effect on the shortening of the dress-skirt in the early 1860s, wearing it with a coloured petticoat and coloured stockings – I well remember the sensation when I first appeared in my new grey silk stockings with red clocks!

My own style has altered from time to time. I certainly wore the crinoline – indeed, was photographed in one of the widest in Paris, with twenty-four steels[6] (this had the advantage that one could do without many underskirts, or even any at all); but though it was said that the Empress herself dealt this fashion the death-blow in January of 1859, when she attended a court ball without a crinoline (a matter which took precedence in the newspapers even over Napoleon's New Year's speech to Baron Hübner!), I believe that I did as much as anyone else to end its predominance, drawing my dresses up over a petticoat and underskirts made of new stuffs and colours – a white dress over a lilac and black petticoat, for instance. I also took to wearing tight sleeves and rich trimmings in place of flounces, though I always kept to low necks, my bosom framed perhaps by a *bertha* of ribbons, *ruches*, laces or embroideries trimmed with flowers; it was my game to allow the neck to fall as low as could be without actually exposing the nipples, and I could not swear that that rule was always strictly kept, at least in exclusively male company (and often I would give dinner parties for men only, on one occasion at a gathering of fifteen men finding only

[6] such a photograph survives in the Enthoven Collection at the Victoria and Albert Museum.

one present to whom I was still a virgin).

It would be a mistake to believe that our influence upon fashion was exerted only at a distance; some of us were consistently seen in the best company. It was Des Varannes who was to claim the honour of first introducing me to His Imperial Highness Prince Napoléon, cousin of the Emperor.[7] He claims that he was talking of me to the Prince one evening when the latter asked him whether he really cared for me, or whether he would agree to introduce us. Des Varannes agreed to do so, and it was as a result of the introduction that I became the Prince's lover.

Nothing could be further from the truth. The introduction had occurred when I was hunting with Prince Achille Murat at Meudon, Napoléon's estate,[8] in I think 1865, and Murat's horse suddenly collapsed under him. Murat was always keen to be in at the kill, whereas I regarded the sport simply as an excuse for riding; so I offered him my mount, which he accepted. No sooner had he ridden off than there was a furious downpour of rain, and I was sheltering under a tree when His Imperial Highness rode up, saw the body of Murat's horse, and heard from me the story. That simple exchange was our introduction; it was not for three years that we met under more intimate circumstances, for although the Prince fell passionately in love with me at first sight, for at least that time I kept him waiting, fanning the flames in order to make them last longer.

When I met him, the Prince was forty years of age. He was not a handsome figure, somewhat plump and with a round and undistinguished face. His family, however, and

[7] Napoléon Joseph Charles Paul Bonaparte, 1822-91, son of Jérôme Bonaparte and Princess Frederika Catherine Sophia von Wurtemburg, and cousin of Napoléon III. Married, in 1859, a daughter of Victor Emmanuel II of Italy. His mistresses included Rachel and Judith, the actresses, and Rosine Stolz, the singer.

[8] which he had inherited from his father, Prince Jérôme, in 1860.

his riches, ensured him a continual stream of handsome mistresses; though to be fair his first affaire when he was a very young boy was with a pretty little baker's wife in Stuttgart. The baker caught them bare behind some flour-bins, and beating the Prince severely threw him into the street naked except for a liberal dusting of flour. This did not discourage him, for his passions were high, and his mistresses later included the famous actress Rachel, the lesser but more beautiful actress Julie Bernat (known as Judith), and various opera singers.

He married, for reasons of policy, Clothilde, [sic] the daughter of Victor-Emmanuel of Italy, who permitted him to make love to her, but was nowhere near spirited enough for him. Though I could not condemn him for looking elsewhere, I must admit that I was somewhat shocked by his total disregard of her feelings, making love with loud exclamations in one room while she and her children dined in the next. But it must also be said that she never showed the faintest signs of disapproval or even of interest. Of course she, poor child, had been brought up in the seclusion of a court (secluded at least for the women), had had no experience of love, and was to learn nothing from the Prince, whose ardour was directed towards other less innocent women. The Princess was perfectly happy with her children (the generation of which was always to me a perfect mystery).

As to the Prince himself, he always treated me with perfect fairness, if not courtesy. He was courteous to no-one, and if his acquaintances complained of the coarseness of his language on public occasions, they should have heard him in private! On the second occasion when we met in the privacy of my rooms, he, having hastily pulled off his clothes, threw himself upon the bed and simply remarked:

'*Dieu, mais je suis fatigué!* I just can't be bothered tonight, Cora; just toss me off, will you?' – the first time that form of insult had been paid to me; and yet he said it with such perfect naturalness that it was clear he spoke the simple truth, so I applied myself to the simple task in hand.

He was certainly by no means nice as a lover; his physical aspect was that of the bull rather than any more refined animal. When dressed, his figure was unattractive – he looked fat, his legs were very short, his neck thick. Without his clothes he was seen to be large rather than fat, and though his trunk was certainly thick, this did not provide the anticipated physical difficulty, for his tool was one of the longest I have ever seen (and as thick as it was long), so that when I rode him (a posture which from choice as well as from convenience we often employed) I at first had to do so with care, for to have sunk fully upon him would have been as dangerous as pleasurable, so that I supported myself by closing my thighs upon the thickness of his torso. Sober, he could contain himself only for a few minutes; but with sufficient brandy could lie for forty minutes without coming off, a circumstance which was upon occasion less admirable than it might have been in someone of a more handsome figure; he also often appeared completely dis-interested, and my part in the proceedings thus became more arduous than amorous.

If I give the impression that he was not my favourite lover, this is not far from the truth as far as physical rapture is concerned; but certainly it is not the case in other directions, for since he received a million francs a year from the Civil List, he was able to provide me with a splendid house in the Rue de Chaillot – at number 101 – which he furnished to his own taste, which proved good enough for me. In another sense, too, he was an entirely suitable lover, for he was entirely lacking in jealousy – a fact which I discovered within two months of our closer acquaintance. After we had been to the theatre and dined, one evening, and returned to my rooms, he had fallen, while still dressed, into a deep sleep from which all my endeavours could not rouse him. Champagne and the opera having prepared me for amorous pleasure, I was unhappy, and let him know so when he woke next morning.

That same evening, we went again to the opera, and this time were accompanied by a member of his household – Lieutenant-de-vaisseau Brunet – and a young friend of his, André Hurion,[9] who had been an actor in a provincial theatre before inheriting a modest fortune from a distant relative and becoming a man of pleasure. They were both men of half the Prince's age; Brunet was one of the most handsome I have ever seen, with very fair hair and a small moustache, an upright slim figure and a charming humour; Hurion, on the other hand, was very dark, somewhat coarser, clean-shaven, and with the most expressive and speaking eyes. They sat on either side of me in the theatre box, where they were most attentive, and afterwards accompanied us to dinner, where I nervously became aware that they were paying me more attention than any man should do when in the presence of a lady's lover. At the end of the meal, when we were drinking our brandy, indeed, Hurion, sitting opposite me, slid his foot up the length of my calf, while handling the stem of his wine-glass in such a manner that no-one could fail to observe his meaning.

At this I rose and suggested that we should leave, whereupon to my surprise Hurion handed me into the

[9] A Lieutenant-de-vaisseau Brunet was at this time attached to the Prince's household; Holden suggests that Hurion may have been *Henri* Hurion, known by the stage-name of Noiret. Both are mentioned in the *Mémoires*, but only as friends of the Prince.

carriage, and he and Brunet climbed in, the Prince accompanying them with no shadow of disapproval! Arrived at my house, they mounted the staircase with us, and accompanied us into my bedroom! By this time some suspicion of what was to occur came to me, and sure enough no sooner was the door shut behind us than the two young men in a moment stripped off their clothing.

'My dear,' said the Prince, 'I am sorry that my conduct last night left you unsatisfied; but as you see I have brought you two of my best beasts, and I hope that they will provide some compensation. Look!' said he, wacking Brunet lightly upon the buttocks with his cane, 'Charles here is fine enough for any filly, while André' (making a gesture in the direction of Hurion's already swelling person) 'has flanks and loins only less formidable than mine own once were. Gentlemen, please don't mind me . . .' At which he took himself off to an armchair with a bottle of brandy and a glass, to watch events.

First the two men with infinite solicitude and many murmurs of appreciation, undressed me. By the time they had completed their task, Hurion's manhood stood out proudly, an enormous tool not as massive perhaps as the Prince's, but evidently much more vigorous and ready for the fray. Sturdy and thick, with the bag beneath supporting two stones of concomitant size, it rose from a belly thickly matted in black, curly hair, the line of which was continued to sprout across his chest. Brunet on the other hand was of a small but perfect frame, so that he looked the very model of a Greek statue, the hair of his body so light that it was almost invisible, lying in tight curls around the root of his tool, which was classically shaped rather than large, an object of beauty which could have failed to attract the admiration only of the insensitive.

To digress, only those women who have had the opportunity of examining a large number of men will know just how their persons vary, one from the other. Some tools are as ugly as the devil; and not necessarily matched with the faces of their possessors. Some are crooked, some straight, some too thin, some too squat; some in repose are pendulous and large so that in excitement they are not much more substantial than at leisure; others can swell from the size of a nut to that of a large fruit, almost in a moment. The same is true of their sensitivity, of course; some at the touch of a finger give up their juices; others are as insensitive as wood, so that the most peculiar attention must be paid to bring them off, even with the utmost compliance of their owners. It has always been a continual cause of curiosity in me to observe these differences, which by the way support none of the familiar old wives' tales – men with large noses can be ill-endowed, while those with thin fingers may have large tools. There is no test other than the ocular.

At first somewhat deterred by the Prince's suavity, when his two friends showed themselves so eager to enjoy me at his command, it would have been ill-natured of me not to show my gratitude for his solicitude. So I led both men to the bed, where they lay one on either side of me, toying with tenderness with my breasts and thighs, while I enjoyed the play of candlelight upon the skin of their bodies, one so dark that it might almost have been that of an Indian, the other utterly pale and white, almost that of a young girl. At last, Hurion placed himself between my thighs and slowly pressed himself into me, filling me with the utmost pleasure. As he moved gently and in a full, plunging motion, he raised his chest so that Brunet could kiss my breasts, running his tongue about my nipples while I stroked his back and buttocks, feeling what I could not see, the light down upon his body. Presently, I felt his fingers as they moved between my body and Hurion's, to caress us both at the extreme point of pleasure.

After a while, careful to afford Brunet the pleasure that his friend and I already enjoyed, I encouraged Hurion to raise himself upon his knees, so that while I still lay impaled, my thighs supported on his own, he was in an upright position, allowing Brunet to throw his leg over and kneel in front of his friend, presenting my lips with the opportunity of embracing him. By this time we were all three at a pitch of pleasure, and within a moment we together reached our goals and spent our passion in mutual delight. So caught up were we that we were equally startled at the applause with which the Prince, observing us from across the room, greeted our endeavours.

We now fell into a pleasant lethargy, and then into a doze; from which, when I woke perhaps an hour later, I saw the chair across the room to be empty, but three glasses of brandy placed upon the bedside table. Waking my two companions, I handed them each a glass, and we toasted our past pleasure and our coming delights, the glass warming us to these, for Hurion immediately took my hand and placed it between his thighs, in the hairy coverts of which a limber something was already astir. A moment's stroking, without even the application of my lips, restored him to full life. Brunet, however, showed no sign of recovery, and even my careful mumbling of his perfect tool had no effect; whereupon to my surprise Hurion bent to do my office with his friend, and the first touch of his tongue performed that office so effectively that Brunet was restored to a pitch of excitement in so brief a time that it was only a moment before I invited him to claim me. Taking my legs behind the knees, the beautiful boy pulled me to the side of the bed, where standing he shot the mark, throwing my legs over his shoulders and leaning his hands behind my head. The perfection of his form had quite a different effect upon me than Hurion's animal strength, and I closed my eyes for a moment in ecstacy when, feeling a tension in Brunet's body, I opened them to see with surprise Hurion's face peering over his friend's shoulder, his hands clutching his forearms, and his body moving in an unmistakable motion. He had entered his friend from behind, and the three of us were moving as one creature. Placing my hands between us, it was with the strangest sensation that I felt two pairs of stones moving in enthusiastic concert, while the ecstatic expressions on my lovers' faces showed that they were fully in accord as to the pleasure of the occasion. I was to learn that Hurion in fact had no special bent towards the enjoyment of boys, nor Brunet towards the enjoyment of women; in fact upon one occasion when at my own request I made love with Brunet alone, I was unable to rouse him sufficiently to employ himself conventionally with me, and it was only by encouraging him to come at me from behind (though still conventionally) that we were able to achieve a conclusion. Both men, however, were so devoted friends that they were willing to support each other in roles which some men would have considered strange or even improper. Upon this occasion, it was the Prince's offer of his services in obtaining promotion for Brunet which had encouraged him to engage his friend on my behalf, which, though he loved him, he knew was his natural bent.

After the mutual thrill had reduced us once more to sleep, we remained unconscious till morning, when my maid bringing me my morning chocolate found the three of us entwined in each other's arms with every aspect of satisfaction; after she had fetched two more cups, and we had breakfasted, Hurion was sufficiently roused to give me one further proof of his admiration, while Brunet merely lay by, tenderly caressing those of his friend's limbs which were available to him. The two young men then took their leave, and I slept until mid-day, when the Prince called to ask solicitously after my night's rest, which I was able to assure him had been entirely restorative, thanking him sincerely for his solicitude.

CHAPTER SIX

The best of protectors – the 'Petites Tuileries' – my golden years – myself as Eve – the finest ball – aristocratic dishabille – New Year's Greetings – the Prince's devotion – the Exposition – Turkish massage – a strange habit – my theatrical triumph – Georges Cavalier – my farewell to the stage – photographed by M. Nadar – and by M. Disderi – with Hurion and Brunet – the Emperor en dishabille – Khalil Bey – his art of love – Gustave Doré – Baron Rogniat – rough and ready.

Prince Napoléon was the most satisfactory, the most generous, the most understanding and amiable of all my protectors. It is not difficult to understand why certain people found him unpalatable. He never suffered pretension kindly, and regarded most members of his family with distaste. He once said to me, quite frankly, 'My cousin,' (the Emperor), 'is a pig; his prefects are a common rabble; and the Government is a load of shit.' He treated the people of Turin with contempt when, at a ball thrown in celebration of his betrothal to the Princess, they failed in his view to give him the honour his position merited. But I myself, and his private secretary Berthet-Leleux, the two who knew him best, regarded him as the finest of men.

Certainly he was happy to maintain me in great style, while at the same time being quite complaisant about my entertaining other, younger men. At one time he made a public show of displeasure at my alliance with a young captain of militia – but that was simply because we were tactless enough to appear together in public, and the Prince had his pride. He was very proud of the 'Petites Tuileries', as my house in the Rue de Chaillot was known; and his visits there, both formal and informal, were an excuse for me to entertain in magnificent style. Indeed, the years between 1865 and 1870 were those of my greatest triumphs; there was no shortage of money, and I spent it freely.

Some have criticized the expenditure of those of us protected by the wealthy, and when some have fallen, latterly, upon lean times, the foolish have asserted that we should have salted away our gold when times were good. But they lose sight of the fact that it is essential, when one is under the protection of a man of good family and of wealth, to mirror that style in which he lives, and to make ostentatious use of his money. A man's wife can afford to appear dowdy and out of fashion; a man's mistress, never, for her appearance is an index of his wealth and pretension. And so it was that I had great parties, was seen night after night at the Maison Dorée, and at Brébant's. My orders were that there was always open house in the Rue Chaillot; even if I was out, no-one was to be refused admittance, and when we returned from the theatre and from dining out, the house would often be full of guests, eating and drinking, sitting on all the available chairs, sprawled on the couches, sitting or lying on cushions on the floor, and even on the beds.

It must not be thought that the house had the air of a brothel. It was simply understood that if a couple felt like making love, they did so, and with the most complete disregard of cardplayers or conversationalists in the same room, who in their turn continued their cards or their talk without taking notice of their companions' activites, or at the most giving them an occasional approving glance.

Neither did they carry tales outside the house, and I have often been in a salon in which half the men were aware that the host had, only the evening previously, consorted in public with a certain woman at that moment taking tea with his wife!

I considered it my duty, since my position was known and recognized by all Paris (including, after all, the Princess) to be seen in public on any notable occasion, and I would take hours to prepare for a grand ball or similar occasion, matching this jewel with that. At fancy-dress balls I tried my best to provide a *petite sensation*, and at first succeeded by the simple device of wearing as little as possible – simply a girdle of tulle about my loins, and jewels carefully disposed. In 1866, the dancers at the ball at the Trois Fréres Provençaux gasped when I appeared as Eve: I wore no jewels at all except for a leaf heavily encrusted with emeralds. The London magazine *Baily's*, from whom a friend later sent me a clipping, said that my 'form and figure were not concealed by any more garments than were worn by the original apple-eater'!

It was in 1866 that there was held at the Ministère de la Marine perhaps the most famous of all modern masked balls. Louis-Napoléon himself attended, dressed as a Venetian nobleman with a magnificent mask, and the main event of the evening was a series of *tableaux vivants* representing the continents. First came four crocodiles with jewels stuck to their backs, and then ten almost naked serving-men even more heavily covered with jewels (which was as well, for they wore little else); then a chariot in which sat the Princess Korsakov, whose limbs had been browned, and who was clothed – or unclothed – with a freedom not often shown in public by aristocrats; in fact she wore only a thin veil of *maillot* through which the lines of her body could be perfectly seen, and which she displayed with the utmost candour. Mlle de Sévres, riding on a camel from the zoo, and accompanied by women attendants with bare breasts and thick wigs of fuzzy black hair, represented Africa. America was represented by a fair-haired woman whom I did not know, and who perhaps no-one knew; she lay perfectly naked in a hammock carried by almost nude negroes, and accompanied by brown men in the feathered headdresses of Indians.

Over three thousand guests attended, vying with each other to show off their jewellery, and many of them so eager to be noticed that even those parts of their bodies which were covered when they arrived were later displayed quite openly. The Marquise de Gallifet came as a swan, but her breast lost its feathers quite early in the evening; the Comtesse de Castiglione, known to be the mistress of the Emperor, and only seventeen,[1] appeared as the Queen of Hearts (the Prince later told me that the Empress' comment was, 'Her heart is a little low!') The ante-chambers became miniature brothels, to which pairs would vanish, to reappear flushed and panting. The Duc de Morny was seen to escort one beauty back into the ballroom, on whose cheek was quite clearly imprinted the pattern of two buttons bearing his coat of arms, and it was noted that the only part of his clothing secured by such buttons was his trousers![2]

New Year's Day was always a spectacular day for me, for it was considered a point of honour to be the first man to call upon me. I always made a point of spending the previous evening with the Prince, so that (since we never retired until after midnight) I could honestly say that the first man I met in the New Year was himself. But he

[1] actually, nineteen
[2] Morny had actually died the year before this ball was held. Presumably the incident occurred on another occasion.

normally left the house before I was awake the next morning, and after I had left my bed and quickly refreshed myself, I would put on a loose gown and return to bed to receive my first caller shortly after eight o'clock.

During the first New Year's Day that I gave this *levée* at the Petites Tuileries, I mistakenly gave way to Prince Gortschakoff's whim that he should be the first man to enjoy my favours in the year 1867. He announced this by placing at my side a box of crystallized chestnuts, each wrapped in a somewhat sticky thousand-franc note, and immediately stripping himself to his shirt. It seemed to me that it would be impolite to refuse him, in view of his kindness; and fortunately the chill morning air, in which he had ridden several miles to visit me, had not impaired his vigour, so that by the time my next visitor was announced he was dressed and gone. Alas, that visitor - Marshal Canrobet - had the same idea, and presented me with a gift of almost equal value. By mid-morning five men had already become my first lover of the New Year, and if I was several thousand francs the richer for it, the morning was somewhat *mouvementé*. In following years, I received visitors on that morning on the strict understanding that their visit was to be platonic. Five men at once, possibly; five men consecutively inevitably provokes a degree of indifference in me.

The Prince's devotion to me was never in doubt. While not jealous, he was certainly inclined to regard my time as his own, and I had to be at pains not to be out of the house, or otherwise employed, when he called (to the extent that one afternoon, when he arrived as I was entertaining Hurion, who had become a close friend, he was in the room before we knew it, and poor Hurion had to descend from the bed and leave the room vainly trying to pack into his drawers his unsatisfied manhood). When the Prince had a spare moment, and I was not with him, he was continually writing me notes professing his adoration, and I am convinced that they were sincere. At the time of the great Universal Exposition, he had his own room built in the exhibition grounds, illuminated with the earliest electric lighting in Paris, of which he was extremely proud. The room was furnished in the style of Turkey, with fine carpets and materials of exotic colour. After walking around the Exposition, looking with interest at the objects on view, the Prince would retire to his room, strip off his clothes and don a dressing-gown, and recline on a low couch, the electric lighting dim behind its shades, while I sat at his side feeding him with sweetmeats – a romantic picture!

The Exposition, in 1867, was a remarkable occasion, with an enormous glass building almost five hundred metres long at its centre, containing exhibits from all over the world – machinery, chemicals, a new cannon designed by Herr Krupp of Prussia, furniture, all manner of things, including paintings and sculpture, clothes and beautiful materials for clothes. One of the sensations was a painting by a M. Manet entitled *Déjeuner sur l'herbe*, which showed a naked woman sitting in a forest glade with some fully dressed gentlemen. The fuss that was made about this painting was absurd, if understandable: many of the people who professed to be disgusted by it must certainly have taken part in such a scene – but being shown it in such reality, and without the masquerade of pretending it to be an antique scene, was too much for them.

The Exposition, or rather its setting, gave great pleasure to those who wished to be outraged; for if the official parts of it were respectable enough, you did not have to go far to find less polite society than crowded the reception rooms and exhibition halls. The Champs-de-Mer, after nightfall, when the lights were lit, resembled an Eastern bazaar. There was plenty of cheap food – you could eat oysters with a bottle of wine for eighty centimes – and this attracted enormous crowds of young men who were not to be contented with the cold nudity of a marble lady lying on top of a lion, which the Emperor had contributed in marble to the Great Pavilion! There were rows of kiosks outside which girls in their national dress performed their national dances – but dances which might have provoked their arrest had they performed them in their native lands, while one suspected also that their dress, or the lack of it, was not the counterfeit of that usually worn in India or in the Pacific islands!

The men naturally besieged these kiosks, and on entering them frequently found no young ladies from the East, but whores from their own districts of Paris, for every manner of prostitute – *cocodés* and *cocodettes, lorettes, petits crevés* – saw the Exposition as a means of making money. The Prince was engaged in showing some of the distinguished visitors around the Exposition, and the Prince of Wales from England, the Pasha of Egypt, the Sultan of Turkey, the King of Sweden, the Tsar of Russia and the brother of the Mikado of Japan were among others not the least of whose interest was in the freedom shown by the ladies of the night. The Prince told me that at the Opéra one night the Prince of Wales, entranced by one of the ballet girls, turned to him and asked 'How much would that one be?' When the Prince told him, Wales, looking gloomy, replied 'Very expensive!', whereupon the Prince said 'Have her on me!' – but never heard that his invitation had been accepted.

A young Turkish nobleman visited the Exposition, and was brought to meet us and to admire the Turkish room, which he did. Next day, he sent around his man, whose

duty was to massage his master in the Turkish style, and
the Prince happily accepted his offer of demonstrating this
exercise. After some persuasion, for it seems that in his
country the ladies are of a more retiring nature than in
Paris, and he was not used to working before them, he
stripped to a cloth about his loins, and produced from a
leather bag a number of oils, each smelling of a different
perfume. The Prince having chosen one of them, the man
then invited him (who had taken off all his clothes) to lie
face downward upon the couch.

The muscular young Turk then filled the palms of his
hands with oil and commenced to stroke, knead and
pummel the Prince's back with the utmost vigour, from the
heels up the thighs to the buttocks, which he made shake
and bounce, and then the shoulders, and pressing so hard
with his thumbs upon the spine that they seemed to
disappear into the flesh. After fifteen minutes or so during
which he not only paid attention to the body, but to the
feet and hands, he instructed the Prince to turn over, and
did the same office to arms, chest, shoulders, belly and
thighs, and at last, with the utmost *sang-froid*, having once
more oiled his hands, took hold of the Prince's tool and
began as it were to milk it, whereupon the Prince immediately sat up and sent the young man perplexedly reeling
back. It seems that it is the habit in Turkey that a massage
should conclude with the discharge of the organ, thus
completing the relaxation of the person; but whether
because he was shy in my presence or because he genuinely
disliked this form of attention, the Prince paid the man
handsomely and sent him away before turning his attention
to me, who speedily achieved the recommended discharge.

I think the Prince was never aware that I sent my maid
the following day to bring the young Turk to the Petites
Tuileries, where he was well paid to exercise his skill upon

me. I was unable to question him, for he spoke little English and less French, but he appeared to be as practised in massaging women as with men, for when the time came, after he had given me the most soothing and beguiling attention, he turned to my sex and with great skill manipulated it to the point of utmost pleasure. As he was doing this, delighted by the muscular thigh only a little way from my lips, I could not resist plunging my hand beneath his loincloth, to pass it over the firm curve of his muscular arse, feel the stones there, and the rampant tool – for surely no man could pay such intimate attention to a lady without arousal. To my amazement, his sex was completely relaxed, limp and unmoved; he smiled at my expression, and calmly taking my wrist, removed my hand to my own side before with his nimble finger bringing me twice in as many minutes to a moving and compulsive paroxysm. It was a strange and most interesting occasion; I can only assume that in his own country ladies are uninterested in persons of a lower class than their own, however adept at love making. I must confess that I was not as satisfied on this occaion as by the full affair, and indeed I have never found it to be so on the rare occasions when other men have similarly treated me.

Among my former acquaintances whom I continued to entertain, discreetly, was Prince Achille Murat, who on one evening in 1866 took me to the Théâtre Bouffes-Parisiens for an operetta. It was an intolerably dull evening – the cast was indifferent, the band poor, and the audience, when not lethargic, was hostile. During the course of the evening, M. Hector Jonathan Crémieux, who ran the theatre (and was part-author with Ludovic Halévy of Offenbach's famous *Orpheus aux Enfers*) came into our box to apologize for the dullness of the performance. We were forced to agree. 'Why,' asked Achille, 'do you not revive *Orpheus?*'

'Do you know,' said M. Crémieux, 'I was thinking of doing so? It is the only thing that can save the theatre. But the problem is, I need someone to play Cupid. It is a small part, but I am convinced that in the right hands it could make a sensation!'

He then left the box, but at the end of the third act, returned, and without preamble asked if I could sing. Of course, I had learned to sing when a small child – M. Crémieux was interested to hear that my father had been a musician – and more than interested, delighted. Nothing would content him but that I should agree to sing the part of Cupid.

Murat was delighted. The first thing he did was to take rooms for me in a house next to the theatre, and to have a special staircase constructed from them down to the stage; he would not hear of my using an ordinary dressing-room, and at all events it would not have been big enough to entertain all those who would wish to visit me after the performances.[3]

The news spread around Paris with the speed of the new electricity! At the first night on January 26, 1867, the theatre was absolutely packed, and many men had paid enormous sums for their seats. French, British, German nobility sat rank on rank, and most of my distinguished rivals were also present – Caro Letessier, Marguerite Bellanger, Giulia Barucci; as well, of course, as the critics.

I had taken care that my first appearance should make an impression: I had almost all my diamonds removed from their settings and sewn to my costume for the occasion, so that it appeared almost to be made of the stones. The Prince had given me an enormous diamond to form the

[3] The *Mémoires* suggest that it was Prince Napoléon who provided these comforts.

arrowhead stuck into my hat, and even the buttons on my bodice were single stones. My first song[4] went well, and from that moment on the evening was my triumph; and after the final can-can (in which I was able to hold my own with the professional dancers) I returned to my suite of rooms to be congratulated by all Paris. I paused only to take off my costume, which my devoted dresser looked after (I later gave Madame Dulac two of the diamond buttons for her trouble), and to put on a loose gown before receiving the congratulations of all my friends, and (if I can judge by looks) of one or two ladies who would willingly have killed me.

The next few weeks were very happy. Most of the critics were kind, and I was delighted when one of them, Paul Foucher, attacked me in public – or rather attacked M. Crémieux for giving the stage to 'a woman famous only for spending money, not perhaps without earning it, but without hiding the way in which she earned it, or even bothering to disguise the names of the men who keep her'. If anyone had needed encouragement to come to the Théâtre des Bouffes-Parisiens, this would have given it them.

Unfortunately, my simplicity was to ruin my good luck. In some ways, I suppose, I was still naïve, for I did not count on the ill-will of certain people, and in particular of one gentleman. I was at the theatre before the thirteenth performance, when someone asked admittance to my private rooms. It was a young man of quite astonishing ugliness, virtually a dwarf, ill-shaped and with a squint and a great hump. Had this creature simply come to admire and to offer good wishes, I would have been happy to have smiled at him and given him my hand to kiss. But no sooner

[4] 'Je suis Cupidon'

was he in the room than he advanced towards me and made as if to snatch at the neck of my gown. I immediately repulsed him, whereupon he announced himself as *Pipe-en-Bois*. This meant nothing to me. He then said that he could put an end to my success, and in the crudest language told me he must have me, there and then, 'on the floor where you belong!' – and made the motions of taking off his trousers.

Happily, at this point Murat came up the stairs and kicked the creature down them. 'But I fear there will be trouble,' he said. The creature was, it seems, one Georges Cavalier, a Left Bank socialist and revolutionary who claimed the censorship of the Paris theatre by being the leader of several *claques*. I learned afterwards that this despicable youth had gone straight to his cronies, the students, and roused them by means of claiming that no foreign actress should be allowed to enjoy succces on their stage. When the curtain went up that evening, no sooner did I make my entrance than whistling and hissing began. I struggled through the performance, but the noise only got worse; though the *fauteuils* applauded, the gallery and upper part of the house persisted in howling me down. By the time the end of the evening came, I had had enough. I decided on one final gesture. I stood by M. Crémieux waiting to join the rest of the company for the final can-can, and just before stepping onto the stage I quickly removed my drawers and handed them to him. The *fauteuils'* applause swelled until the din of the students could no longer be heard; in the gallery, of course they could not see the *revolutionary* effect of my *dishabille*! When I came on to take my bow, the lower part of the house rose to me (quite literally, in the case of some gentlemen, Murat later told me!), and the students seemed to stop their howling, enraged at my success. To rub the lesson in, I turned my back and, bowing, threw my skirts over my back and made a certain gesture which my days in the main streets of the city had taught me. As the curtain fell I heard the roar of laughter from downstairs competing with the enraged bellow from above. M. Crémieux, though apparently disapproving, could not help laughing as I passed him. I held out my hand to him to reclaim my drawers, but he shook his head and tucked them inside his waistcoat as, he said, a souvenir of my last appearance at the Théâtre des Bouffes-Parisiens. Indeed it proved to be so, though I think I can claim to have won the day, and Crémieux often begged me to return. Murat provided a *corps* of men to see me home that evening, and Marie Petit, who had sung the part before, took it over.

Next morning I woke in my bedroom at the Petites Tuileries, early, to hear singing under my window. I looked out, and there were one or two of my escort of the previous night, still on duty, and singing a song which was to be the rage of Paris for several weeks:

> Comme l'Hélène des Troyens
> Que, grâce à Paris, on renomme,
> Hier aux Bouffes-Parisiens
> Cora Pearl a reçu la pomme![5]

It was not long after my appearance at the theatre that I received a message from a M. Gaspard Felix Tournachon, who in 1853 had opened a photographic studio in Paris. I had been photographed once or twice before, but never by so distinguished a man as M. Tournachon, who called himself Nadar, and was by far the best-known photographer in the city, and who had made pictures of Louise

[5] Like Helen of Troy/Renamed, thanks to Paris/Yesterday at the Bouffes-Parisiens/Cora Pearl took the apple!

Philippe, Delacroix the painter, Rossini the composer, and Dumas the writer. I was delighted. I went to his studio and he photographed me in riding clothes and in several dresses.[6] Unfortunately, when I asked him for his fee, he revealed that it was I who was supposed to pay him, whereupon I left; I have never seen the photographs, and I can only suppose that he destroyed them.

A happier experience occurred a few weeks later, when another young photographer, M. Disderi, came to the Petites Tuileries and offered me a large fee if I would pose for him. I happily agreed, and he came a few days later with his machine. He took several photographs of me in various dresses, and then asked me to remove all my clothes, which I did. He posed me in various positions of a less revealing sort, but gradually, as I noticed, became bolder, finally asking me to caress myself, which I declined to do. He asked whether it would not be possible for me to pose with a gentleman? The photographs, he assured me, would only be disposed of very expensively, they would not circulate among the lower classes, and would not be in the least demeaning; he also asked whether I did not think it an honour to have my picture made while employed in an occupation of which I was by far the most expert and beautiful practitioner?

After a brief discussion of fresh terms, I agreed, and sent a messenger for Brunet, whose fair hair and white body would most perfectly complement my own. He came around, nothing loath; he was a vain fellow. Unfortunately, though he removed his uniform with alacrity, it soon became clear that without the attentions of his friend

[6] No photographs of Cora Pearl signed by Nadar are to be found, although one has survived of her in riding costume, seated upon a rocking-horse.

Hurion he would not be able to rouse himself to a state of enthusiasm suitable to the poses M. Disderi required; time and again, by one means or another, I tried to persuade his head to rise, but although once or twice I succeeded, we had to maintain our position for some time while the photograph plate was exposed, and after fifteen seconds or so his tool would relapse, so that the photographer was in despair. Finally, I sent for Hurion as the only solution, and while we waited for him we posed in various positions which disguised the fact the Brunet was limp as a small peas-pod (though M. Disderi properly enthused about the proportions of the rest of his body, and was happy to photograph the play of light upon his back and buttocks – indeed, was so enthusiastic that I suspected his motives at last, and indeed Brunet seemed hopeful that the photographer might continue his attentions after the photographs were taken).

When Hurion arrived and stripped himself, there was no more difficulty – except that M. Disderi declined to take photographs of the three of us, explaining that there was little demand for such photographs among the ladies (for he told us that these photographs sold chiefly to ladies, for the men, he said, could get the real thing and were not interested in pictures – not, I must say, my own experience entirely). Finally, by toying and caressing, Hurion would get Brunet to stand, and then when we were posed, would situate himself at the side of the camera, his magnificent equipment fully extended, and by means of lascivious gestures, toying with himself and the like, kept Brunet up to the mark. M. Disderi then took some photographs of Hurion and myself at work, and, after some difficulty in persuading Hurion to leave me, of the two men (which I would not have found attractive, but which the photographer enthused upon).

The business over, we took tea, and I enquired whether

M. Disderi would not care to retire with me, for I thought that perhaps a certain shyness had restrained him from making an approach, and the care he had taken with the photographs (as well as the fee he paid) seemed to require some kindness. He said however that he always found that manipulation of the camera was so difficult a matter that he was able only to concentrate on the necessary lighting, et cetera, and excused himself. Brunet then said he had to go to his duty, and the two men left together, while Hurion, who had been aroused to such a pitch as to need relief, retired with me to bed where we satisfied each other with no difficulty. Again, I never saw copies of any of the photographs, and although the Prince once brought me a scene of two men in congress, the heads of which were disguised (which often happened) but whose bodies were unmistakably those of my friends, this was *not* one of the photographs taken in my house, for the background was different; I imagine that Hurion and Brunet found a pleasant additional source of income with their new friend.

The speedy growth of interest in photography over the next few years resulted in a large number of such photographs; many men bought and operated their own cameras. Indeed de Morny had been something of a photographer and I posed for him on one occasion. As we lay languidly upon a couch after he had enjoyed me, he asked if he could photograph me 'for his collection' – producing a walnut box which, unlocked, proved to contain forty or fifty photographs, all of women, naked, some extremely well known, usually with a wreath of flowers placed to conceal their secret part. Upon the backs of these were marked not only the name of the subject, but a number; and in the same box were an equal number of screws of paper, similarly numbered, and containing tufts of hair, unadorned with flowers!

I agreed to be photographed, but instead of accepting the

small bunch of flowers which the Duc handed me, insisted on placing there instead a small frame containing a photograph of the photographer! – who afterwards cut a little hair from my person himself, with a small pair of gold scissors kept in a kid purse in the walnut box. I wonder what happened to that box, for the Duc was dead within the year . . .

I met M. Nadar once more – in court, for he was appointed court photographer, and I occasionally saw him as the Prince was escorting me to his rooms. Nadar bowed coldly, seeming to fail to recognize me![7] I never appeared officially at court, thought I was once introduced to the Emperor by the Prince, who informed me that his Majesty was eager to tread where his distinguished subjects had trodden, as he somewhat tactlessly put it. The Emperor had slept with various women, among them Marguerite Bellanger and La Castiglione, but, observing protocol, none of them would talk about him, except that he had told them he 'enjoyed a woman as he enjoyed a good cigar'. This did not seem to me to promise a great deal, and in fact our single meeting was soon over; for he strode into the room, late at night after a state dinner to which I was not invited, threw off his breeches (though no other part of his dress) and hurled himself upon me without a word, discharging within a few moments, rolling over, and immediately going to sleep. He was already ill and in pain at the time, which must excuse him.

Two or three years later, I found myself alone with Marguerite, his most constant mistress, who remained faithful to him for many years and is said to have borne his child. I asked whether she had found her duties arduous,

[7] Many years later it was Nadar who confirmed to Bettina von Hutton, author of *The Courtesan* (1933), that Cora Pearl had been, briefly, the mistress of the Emperor, though Cora denied it in the *Mémoires*.

and she smiled in such a manner that it was clear he had been no more demanding with her than with me. Such a lover would not suit me; but the explanation is, I think, that Marguerite was of a cooler temperament, who did not need male company and male solace to the extent I did; she was happy in her own style, and an occasional bout with Napoléon in his boots satisified her without making her wish for any other attention.

It has been a cause of astonishment to me to note how many women have claimed to have been His Majesty's whore: Alexandrine Vergeot, Virginia Oldini, La Barucci . . . it only proves that some women put 'honour' above satisfaction! The Prince and I often used to laugh about his cousin's lack of finesse, for though the Prince was by no means insatiable, he loved to see me enjoying myself, and certainly never during the whole time of our acquaintance came to bed in his boots, or indeed wearing anything other than the night attire he put on when he did not wish to make love.

It was the Prince who introduced me to Khalil Bey, who had taken a box at the Bouffes-Parisiens for my first night, and who was related to the Turk who had brought his masseur to the Exposition. Khalil Bey was immensely rich, and entertained extensively. He was a perfect host, although with some strange habits – viz, he would receive his guests in winter in the gardens, while in summer he received them inside the house! But that house had every comfort: on my first visit, I was led not to his rooms, but to a bathroom with a vast pool of marble containing warm, scented water, where I was to bathe, then to a room where I presumed he would present himself. Yet he did not, and after a while I fell asleep and slept for an hour in the warm, scented air before being awakened by the sound of a flute, as Khalil himself entered. He was then a man of well over sixty years, but lean and handsome, not fleshy, and with the expertise in love so often possessed by the Eastern peoples, and so well set out in *The Scented Garden* (a translation of which came to Paris from Algeria some years ago, and which offers an extensive education to the young man and woman alike).[8]

Khalil Bey was able to satisfy me as thoroughly as any man I have known, and much more thoroughly than many of half his age. Indeed, on several occasions, having made love to me for well over two hours, he still possessed himself in a standing state, and seeing me quite exhausted with pleasure, withdrew himself, covered me with silk and left me. I asked him whether he was not himself unsatisfied; whereupon 'No,' he said, 'for we believe that emission is a signal of defeat rather than of triumph,' and intimated that he felt all the pleasure of a discharge without the mechanical signs. The art, he said, was one called by the Indians *Tantra*.

Khalil left Paris when we had spent his fortune, saying that he would return when he had made a second; but Paris never saw him again.

It was in the spring of 1868 that I met an artist whose name has now become familiar and who was even then beginning to be known – Louis Auguste Gustave Doré. He was introduced to me by a friend who advised me on buying pictures, and was at that time working on illustrations for the English poet Tennyson's verses about King Arthur.[9] He was a serious, intense fellow in his thirties, who had already drawn the pictures for works by Dante and Milton, but that this had not made him too solemn was demon-

[8] Presumably this was the book better known to us as *The Perfumed Garden*, translated from the French in 1886 by Sir Richard Burton, who had found it in Algeria.
[9] *Idylls of the King*; Doré's edition was prepared during 1867-8.

strated by the fact that when we first met he remarked:
'Ah, the lady whose breasts are reputed to be the shapliest
in Paris. May I be permitted to draw them?'

Whereupon I made an appointment, and the following
day went to his studio, where I posed for him (and I may
say, have recognized my breasts as those of many a Biblical
heroine since!) He became very silent as he drew me, and at
last laid down his pencil, came over to me, and without
more ado began to press kisses upon me, whereupon I
returned them with interest, for he was a fine and intelligent man, who soon turned out to be as well-shaped and
well-equipped as some of the heroes of his less public
drawings, commissioned by, among others, the Prince.

We continued to meet for two years, and at one time he
continually pressed me to marry him; but the idea of
marriage has never commended itself to me, and we
continued as lovers. He was always particularly passionate
when we first met; but after one or perhaps two bouts
would go for his paper and pencils and sketch me; he made
several sketches of my most intimate parts which were in
detail the finest I have seen; but he would never leave them
with me, and I have often wondered what occurred to
them.

Doré was, in the variety of his conversation, the lightness
of his spirits, the invention of his amorous attentions, the
loving appreciation of my company, one of the most
charming men I have known, and had I been of a more
settling disposition – or less convinced that marriage is a
recipe for boredom and eventual neglect – who knows but
that I might have become Madame Doré? But it was not to
be, and eventually, becoming weary of the clandestine
nature of our relationship (which he concealed from his
growing company of patrons) we parted, not without
regret. I gave him a photograph of myself, in remembrance,

which I am told he still treasures.[10]

I had no wish to send Doré away. The Baron Abel Rogniat was another matter. I had met him in my dressing-room at the theatre, and taken pity on him as a young man who had antagonized his family by his obstinate behaviour, and had little money. He was somewhat prepossessing, and looked at me so adoringly and so hopelessly that I intimated that he could call upon me in a day or two. No sooner had I arrived home that night, however, than he appeared, undressed himself, and offered to come to bed. Unfortunately beneath a polished exterior he proved to be dirty and unwashed, and not to be polite, smelled of the farmyard. I therefore invited him to bathe himself; he only consented if I would wash him, which I was forced to do or to take the risk of a scandal by having him thrown into the street.

Rogniat proved almost worth washing, for if he had the manners of a goat he also had something of that animal's virility. In fact, recently having been a little too exclusively pampered by young men of aristocratic and sophisticated tastes, and by the Prince and by Murat, neither of whom had much stamina, I found Rogniat's rough and ready approach – butting me with all the finesse of an animal at rut – somewhat pleasurable. Alas, I was not prepared for his settling into my house as if it were his own. I had eventually to threaten him with the Prince and the Army if he would not leave; whereupon he picked up a whole cabinet of china and hurled it to the ground, saying that he would kill himself and his death would be at my door.

Finally I persuaded him – partly by an excess of amorous attention and partly by repeated assurances of the danger-

[10] At an exhibition in Paris in 1948, such a photograph (inscribed 'Remember. C.P.') was exhibited as once having been the property of Doré.

ous quality of the Prince's jealousy, who I explained was inclined to hire ruffians to castrate those with whom I was unfaithful to him (poor Plon-Plon[11] would have been outraged at the thought!) – to leave my house, Paris and indeed the country. He went to Spain to look after some family mining interests, although I was to meet him again in other circumstances.

[11] This is the only occasion in this book in which Cora Pearl calls Prince Napoléon by the nickname by which he was commonly known in France.

CHAPTER SEVEN

A dishonourable lover – a restful interlude – pleasantly interrupted – innocence refined – a sad farewell – a new fashion – Comte Aguado – Loulou at work – equestrian portraits – startling sacrifice to art.

I must not give the impression that all my lovers were honourable men, though they were certainly almost all to some degree entertaining. I was approached in the Bois one morning, while riding, by a handsome and dashing young man who gained my attention simply by riding his horse alongside my carriage and with a spectacular leap taking his place at my side, while his horse cantered off! He introduced himself as the Prince de Hersant, formerly of the Serbian Army, and now in Paris because of a family quarrel. He asked only for the pleasure of my company while riding; but his definition of the word riding turned out to be very much what I would have supposed, and what in fact I welcomed, for he was a gentleman of spectacular accomplishments in whatever kind of saddle.

Within a few days we were regularly making excursions to the Ville d'Avray and St Cloud, returning tired to my rooms afterwards where we would bathe together before taking our leisure in bed. The Prince had a hard, muscular body, and used it like the finest of instruments, bringing me again and again to a pitch of pleasure which I by no means always experienced with other lovers.

He did not shower me with gifts; indeed, unlike almost any other man I had met within five or ten years, he gave me nothing but himself. And in fact one day as we lay bathed in the dews of each other's perspiration, he told me he had unfortunately lost fifteen thousand francs. He did not say how, but I imagined, at gaming. He did not ask me whether I could lend him money, but reaching out to the drawer at the side of my bed, I covered his body with bank notes, some of which were rather badly damaged by the ensuing action. He refused to leave me that night, and in fact took up residence in my rooms for a fortnight, during which we went out only on our rides. On the fifteenth day, he went out alone, while I was still asleep, and never returned. He took with him not only the notes,[1] but a valuable jewel which the Prince had given me; and when I made discreet enquiries he turned out to be quite a well-known rogue. It is perhaps a mark of my naïvety that I had thought that no such one would dare to approach *me*; but he was cheap at the price of a gift!

My other experience of that year – which I think must have been 1868 – was a more pleasant and lengthy one. In the summer I shut up the Paris house and went out to the Château, making it known that I wished to spend a month or two alone. I told the Prince that I would send a message when he could come to me, but that I would be grateful to be left alone till then. He obviously believed that I had found some new lover; in fact, I had not – it was simply that I had not been completely alone for some years, and felt in need of a little rest.

For three weeks I spent my time idly, strolling in the grounds down by the river Loiret, which wound past my house and through the little village of Olivet before joining the Loire itself outside Orléans, lying in bed as long as I liked – and alone! – in the mornings, eating when I pleased

[1] 15,000 francs, according to the *Mémoires*

and sleeping when I pleased. Sometimes I lay down in the arbour by the backwater in the morning sun, under the shade of a parasol, and dozed, only the splash of the water and the calls of the birds to disturb or lull me. I did so one morning in mid-June, when suddenly, half-awake, I had the feeling that I was being overlooked. Opening my eyes, I saw silhouetted against the sun a small figure in the lower branches of a tree not far away, half hidden in the thick leaves. I lay for a while and watched. The figure was quite still and intent upon me, as I lay with my head on my arm. It was, I thought, a boy. I called out to him not to be afraid, to come down and talk – I was a little lonely, if the truth be told, after some time with only the servants for company, and a village urchin would be a pleasant and unusual companion.

He swung for a moment from a branch, dropped to the ground, and nervously approached. Indeed he was an urchin, dressed virtually in rags through which a dark bronze skin appeared through many rents and gaps. He stood with his hands behind his back and still stared unflinchingly at me. He came, he said, from Noras, on the outskirts of the village, and had regularly climbed over the wall since he had been 'a child' – he was not much more now! He liked, he explained, the apples and peaches which grew in the gardens, and he liked watching the ladies and gentlemen. Thinking of some of the recreations enjoyed by my guests, I imagine he found them very interesting indeed.

'Well, come here and sit, and we'll talk,' I said. He sat down at my side, his old shirt slipping off one shoulder as he lent on his elbow, an enchanting picture with a mop of curly dark hair falling low on his forehead, and his slender bare feet burrowing into the grass. We talked for an hour; he told me about his games and adventures, the games and adventures of childhood, and asked me about life in Paris, where of course he had never been. Finally, dimly in the distance the clock of St Marceau chimed, and he sprang to his feet. 'May I come tomorrow?' he asked, and we arranged to meet at the same hour.

As I approached the river next afternoon, I heard a splashing, and as I reached the bank saw my young friend striking out towards me, grinning happily. He waved, ducked his head in the water, and spluttered happily. Without a second thought I threw off my clothes and joined him in the dark, cool water. We splashed and ducked each other like childhood friends, chased each other, shouted and laughed; he dived to swim beneath me, and I felt his slim naked body slide between my legs before he surfaced in front of me to grin again with pleasure.

After a while, we climbed out of the water, and I was pleased to see that he showed no embarrassment at our being naked; though after all he must have seen enough naked men and women there before, from his vantage-points in the trees and reeds. We threw ourselves down on the grass in the hot sun to dry off, and unselfconsciously he snuggled up to me, his head on my arm and his own arm thrown across my waist. There we dozed innocently in the warmth, our skins drying and the little sparkling drops of water gradually disappearing from our bodies.

I woke from a doze to find him, his head raised, looking closely at my breast, his finger stretched out as though to touch the nipple. He caught my eye. I smiled, at which he reached his hand further and brushed the nipple with the tip of his finger, then ran it round and down the curve of the breast. A flush of blood filled the flaccid tip, and it rose under his very eyes, which made him chuckle with glee, and I could feel against my thigh the stirring of his little tool. I could not help tightening my arm along the length of his back, cupping one small tight buttock in the palm of my hand, which it seemed to fit like a ball into its socket. With, I suppose, the natural male instinct, he bent his head and rubbed my nipple with his lips, then opening his mouth fixed upon it with a child's instinct, as his hand glided down over my belly to the hair at its base. For a while we lay still as he sucked at my breast like a baby; but his body was not the body of a baby.

I hesitated whether kindly to repulse him. But he was no child; he was at least fourteen or fifteen, and his innocence was only the innocence of a happy young animal, not that of a carefully nurtured town boy, whose instincts are betrayed as soon as he can speak by the politesse of his family circle. I reached over and stroked his beautiful young body, from the armpit down the side of the chest, then the rise of the hip, then the muscular little thighs; and then pushed him gently away so that he fell on to his back, and I could see his smooth chest, hairless but well developed, a miniature of a man's, his small round belly marked by its deep navel, and below it something very different from the tiny cord-like appendage which I had noticed as we left the water: fully risen so that it lay back along his belly, lifting the stones beneath into a tight parcel, his tool would no doubt grow yet bigger, but was obviously no longer merely a convenient but a lustful organ.

He must have thought, as I leant for a while merely looking, that I was rejecting him, for half unconsciously his hand stole to his tool and began to rub at it; but I reached out smiling, took his hand by the wrist, and placed it at my waist. 'No need for that, my child,' I told him. His eyes opened wide with happy speculation, and I reached out and took his tool in my own hand, feeling how strongly the muscle there beat against my palm.

I realized of course that no lad of his age would be capable of retaining himself for long; so I lay back, opened my thighs, and lifted his light body between them, so that the deep tanned brown of his torso was strongly contrasted to the white of mine. He wriggled against me like a fish, and I felt his tool fruitlessly struggling to gain entry through my navel! I reached down and guided him into me, whereupon he closed his eyes until they wrinkled, and wriggled still more, before beginning to buck like a young colt, for perhaps half a minute, then I felt the muscles of his whole body contract and shudder, and he lay still. He opened his eyes again and looked into mine, grinning happily. I closed my legs and arms around him and hugged him, feeling as happy as though I had been myself in ecstacy in the arms of my first lover.

He struggled free, drew himself up, and sat astride me, looking down in wonder at his tool, which was still erect, a little pearl at its end. He put his small hands on my breasts, leant over, and kissed me on the cheek like a friend or a relative, and made to climb off. I put my hands on his hips and held him. 'Not so fast, my friend,' I said; 'one thing you must learn is that you don't leave a lady unsatisfied!' His puzzled look showed that his knowingness, as I imagined, extended only as far as observation had taught him, and that that had been more excited than real.

The regenerative power of youth can never be over-estimated. Within a minute or two he was eager to continue his education. Since he was too small to satisfy me in the conventional attitude, I made him lie on his back and knelt astride him, teaching him to excite me with his hands as I moved very gently upon him. At first he showed a tendency to maul me like a housewife kneading dough, but he was a quick study, and within an hour was handling me as gently at any lover of superior years and experience. The time passed like a flash before he had to leave, sworn to silence, and to return next day.

For the next five weeks we spent every afternoon together. He was insatiable, and apart from the pleasure such a young lover gave me by his enthusiasm and natural love of the sport, I took pleasure in educating him in the ways of love. Having watched my guests from an even more tender age, he was eager to experiment with all the postures he had seen, although not all of them could he manage without assistance. For instance, when he wished to take me from behind, he was quite unable to reach, and finally was forced to kneel upon the trunk of a fallen tree before he could thrust to the mark! He had always been, from five years old, he told me, a collector of birds' eggs, and this perhaps had taught him to use his hands with the utmost delicacy, which, once informed that the lightest touch was often more ingratiating than the more violent, he did upon me with an expertness which was soon capable of bringing me to the point of ecstacy. It may have been, too, that the care he took in blowing his eggs, to crack or break which was a tragedy, gave his lips that suppleness which made him almost the best lover conceivable from that respect. He had not, from his vantage points, been able to see the details of such love-making, and to teach him to use his tongue well was a happy endeavour; the sweetness of his own body made it a pleasure to feed upon him, too, for his body tasted like honey to my lips and tongue, though I must admit that I took the habit of bringing soap and towels to the river with me, for batheing was with him a habit of pleasure rather than cleanliness.

The idyll ended as strangely as it had begun. As always, my servants knew perfectly well about our meetings – or so I thought – and as always followed my instructions as to discretion. One of my footmen always brought tea for myself and milk for the boy down to the river, leaving it on a table in an arbour nearby. One afternoon, Colette, one of the maids, brought the tray down instead of the footman. Lazily, I saw her approaching over the grass as I lay with my back against a hummock, the boy with his head in my lap, his legs spread out in the sunshine, and my hand negligently lying over his thigh. When the girl was within a few yards of me, and just about the turn to the arbour, she let out a shriek of astonishment and anger and dropped the tray. The boy raised his head, stared, then jerked away from me to crouch at my feet.

To cut a long story short, the boy whom I had thought came from the village was in fact the maid's son,[2] who had grown up in a house of his grandmother not far away, but had been sneaked into the grounds by his mother since he was a small child, and told always to keep out of my sight. Colette was furious with the boy, and furious and frightened at the same time as she taxed me with 'seducing' him. This of course was ridiculous, but, making allowances for a mother's feelings, I gave her a generous gift of money when dismissing her, and threatened that if I should hear of anything ill happening to young Marcel (as he was called) she should certainly hear of it. Happily, his father had been a soldier who had long passed out of their lives, so there was no question of his being beaten – he was of an age which would have made that a difficulty for his mother.

The night after I turned the girl away, Marcel either bribed or forced her to let him into the château and show him the way to my room; he had come, he said, to thank me for what I had taught him, and did so, since he had nothing else to give me, by showing me his skills, which I must

[2] Marcel Driou, an elderly man who lived in La Source, near Orléans, between the wars, used to claim that he had had just such an experience in his youth at the Château Beauséjour; but at the same time that he was in fact Cora Pearl's illigitimate child, although there is no evidence that she ever had one.

confirm did demonstrate me to be a fine teacher in the art I had studied most completely. At first light, before the house was stirring, I woke from sleep to find him kneeling over me, studying my every feature with the most perfect attention; he then very tenderly took me for the last time, while I was half asleep, seeming like a young faun with his brown skin and long hair; then he drew his loose trousers and shirt over that magnificent young body, and slipped from the room. The next day, the Prince arrived, and it was not without a feeling of the contrast that I saw him approach me that night, his giant thighs and great belly shaking, and felt my hands almost sink into the soft flesh of his shoulders as he cumbersomely climbed upon me to spend himself once and for all after three or four thrusts. The gift of a magnificent necklace of sapphires somewhat, but not altogether, consoled me; it was some months, however, before the memory of Marcel left me – indeed, I might admit that it has never entirely vanished.

I returned to Paris in the autumn to start a new fashion. I was already notable for painting my face and altering the colour of my hair. While I was with Marcel, I had foolishly (as I thought) ignored my usual habit of keeping my body well covered from the sun; batheing and lying in the sun afterwards had resulted in my entire body being coloured, even the insides of my thighs (exposed to the sunlight as I lay with the boy's head between them) and the undersides of my breasts. The Prince had been surprised but not unattracted by this, and obviously spread the word about, for soon I began to notice that the ladies of Paris society no longer had the snow-white shoulders and breasts of former years, and a sun-coloured skin became, if only briefly, the fashion.

The Comte Aguado, a rich Spaniard, was the first man other than the Prince to discover how far the sun-brown

covered my body. He was announced one morning at the
Paris house, and came in leading a little Havana bitch. His
valet, he informed me, had been told by the milkman that I
had a Havana dog whom I would perhaps permit to
impregnate his bitch, from whom he was eager to breed.
My new maid, Clapotte, who had an air of great modesty,
had not been able to get from him his business, but in my
presence his tongue was loosened. Discovering that his
bitch was in season, I had Loulou brought to me. (On
hearing the name the Comte wondered whether a mistake
had been made, but I was able to show him that he need
have no worry, and Loulou confirmed my statement by
leaping with enthusiasm upon his bitch, with whom he was
soon tied in a love bond.)

The Comte asked whether a fee was demanded; finding
him, with his dark looks and lithe figure, an attractive man,
I remarked that the only fee I would accept from his bitch's
master was the kind of fee that Loulou was now paying.
The Comte seemed somewhat surprised, but permitted me
to show him my bedroom, where he was not slow to prove
an enthusiasm that matched my little dog's, though I am
glad to say with more finesse than Loulou was capable of.
Strangely, perhaps inspired by the dog's performance, he
favoured the canine approach to such an extent that he
would adopt no other, and since I find all fours, though a
stimulating posture, one which is tiring after a few hours,
our liaison was not a long one. On our second meeting,
however, while his belly was knocking against my arse and
his stones beating my thighs, he hung a magnificent
necklace of pearls about my neck; another time he presented a splendid pair of diamond ear-rings, so that I was
able to bear with equanimity the fact that I was never to
have the pleasure of looking into his eyes as my ecstacy and
his occurred – a thing which never fails to give me warm

satisfaction. The Comte was a gentleman in the full sense of the word, and my sudden desire towards him fully justified; he was as generous as his reputation suggested.

Loulou performed his task excellently, and the Comte's bitch pupped before he left Paris, recalled to Spain (he was in the diplomatic service). Poor Loulou was to expire in Rome some years later, when I made the mistake of dyeing his hair blue to match a new dress; something in the dye unfortunately disagreed with him. Happily, a photograph reminds me of him.

I always wished to have some memento of my pets, and it was soon after the Comte's disappearance that I engaged the painter François Emile de Lansac to paint me on horseback; in fact, he painted two versions, inspired by a pair of paintings by the Spanish artist Goya. In one, I was fully dressed in riding clothes, sitting side-saddle and facing the onlooker. In the second painting I was in precisely the same posture, but naked, the riding crop in my right hand lying along my thigh; the horse was without saddle or harness, too, its mane tangled at a point with my own as I lifted my right leg so that my foot hung by its neck.[3]

The horse was the darkest of mares, and my sun-browned body caught and reflected the highlights of her beautiful hide. M. Lansac was truly inspired, and indeed his painter's smock could scarcely contain or constrain his excitement, which I offered early in the proceedings to satisfy, thinking that perhaps the painting would suffer; but he explained that his own excitement would be transmitted in his work, as indeed it was, for I noticed that few gentlemen could regard it without paying the same tribute as the painter. They were more ready, in general, to satisfy

[3] There is a record only of the first painting, which was sold for only 300 francs after Cora Pearl's death in 1886. It has since vanished.

themselves by a close acquaintance with the subject than was the artist – the sacrifices made to art are sometimes of an intensity to stagger belief. The painting, alas, vanished from my Paris house during the days of the Siege, when I was out of the city.

CHAPTER EIGHT

The Siege of Paris – lovers' farewells – evacuation of my stables – France a republic – Rogniat again – an expressive man – excessive boredom – Gambetta's escape – Hurion and Brunet – a convenience of Army life – Hurion disagrees – inconvenience of cold weather – enervating effect of hunger – my house a hospital – salutary effects of love on the patients – a British visitor removed – the opportunity of escape – a balloon journey – escape well celebrated – I leave for England.

I find myself in some difficulty when I come to describe the war of 1870–1 and the Siege of Paris, for to be completely frank I am no politician and could never understand how it was that not long after all Paris had joined to *fête* King Wilhelm of Prussia at the time of the Exposition, accompanied as he was by the magnificent Bismarck in his grand white uniform with a great white eagle on his shining helmet, it suddenly happened that France declared war! Crowds immediately filled the streets of the city chanting *'Vive la guerre!'* and even singing the *Marseillaise*, which had not been openly heard there for many years.

Of course it was a matter for me to support the current feeling, which I did by immediately donating a large sum to the fund started by *Le Figaro* to send every soldier in the Army a glass of brandy and a cigar; my name was prominently printed towards the head of the list of subscribers. For a few days, business was lively in the common houses of Paris, for every young man believed that it would soon be his duty to enlist, and wished to say farewell to the pleasures of the bedroom before he did so. I myself received several of the younger members of the aristocracy, and was amused to find that even those whom I knew to be, normally, considerate and even tender lovers were now preoccupied almost entirely by the number of times they could be raised to the supreme moment of passion in a single night, as though they wished to make the most of what might be their last opportunity. I could not believe that so many young men would be slaughtered, and took the generous presents which they left me without compunction. (One of these, by the way, come with a note which read: 'Farewell, dear Madame, a long farewell, and my best wishes to all your husbands!')

It soon became clear that I had been unduly optimistic; a note of hysteria was heard in the city at the news of a supposed *debâcle* at Sédan; one moment the streets were full of cheering, rejoicing men and women – the next there was weeping and wailing; one day the streets were decked with flags and coloured lights – the next, down came the flags and out went the lights! Finally came the news that there had indeed been a great defeat, and a strange gloom settled over Paris, people wandering pointlessly here and there, gathering in small groups to talk quietly about the possiblity of losing the war, gathering beneath lamp-posts to read by the yellow light the latest newspaper dispatches. For the first time I heard open talk of deposing the Emperor and proclaiming a republic.

It was at this moment that I began myself to take certain precautions. First, it was necessary to look after those creatures who could not look after themselves. Realizing that with the advance of the Prussian army Paris might soon be threatened, I told one of my grooms to take eight of my best horses outside the city as though for exercise, then to make off for Beauséjour as swiftly as possible. He did so, and I afterwards heard that these horses were among the last to leave Paris; a fortunate thing for them, indeed, for they would certainly have found their way eventually into the starving stomachs of the *bourgeoisie*.

It was astonishing to me, when I considered it, that anything could have made its way through the crush on the roads into the city, packed as these were with carriages and carts and crowds of people on foot, trying to escape, as they thought, to the safety of the capital. Countrymen made their way into the protection of Paris, often with cartloads of cabbages and leeks which they were determined should not fall into the hands of the enemy. Amazed at the sight of people coming into the city when it was obviously better to leave it, I instructed my servants to buy certain foods and store them up, salting meat and placing it in the cellars, and preserving what fruit could be preserved. I thought of leaving for Beauséjour; but I have always been tempted to participate in any excitement which offers, and there was an air of excitement about life in Paris that late summer which was irresistible to me. By the middle of September, the city was a fortress, almost every man to be seen in its streets carrying his own gun. By now, too, the Second Empire had ended, and we were a Republic; a mob had broken into the Tuileries and sacked it, and the eagles carved in stone on the outside of the building had been defaced and knocked off; young men in red caps climbed the lamp-posts and sang the *Marseillaise* from their tops, and there was such rejoicing that one would have thought a new epoch of safety and plenty had been proclaimed, rather than the end of luxury and pleasure and the beginning of hardship.

I cannot say that the end of the Empire was of great concern to me. I had of course some friends who were of the aristocracy, and protectors high in its superior families;

but none of them, and I must include the Prince and indeed the Emperor, seemed to me naturally equipped for the leadership of a great nation. Indeed, no woman who has experience of the behaviour of most men in the bed-chamber can have much confidence of their behaviour as leaders, nor in my experience do they behave more ration-ally in the latter capacity than in the former. It would no doubt be a matter of fact that I would lose, financially, should the great families in society be bereft of their incomes and estates; but I was then quite confident that whoever ruled, I would remain capable of making my living. So was I also confident of my physical safety, in all the destruction and excess. Happily, I had friends at every level of society, and indeed the mob never attempted me any harm – which I was to repay by remaining in Paris throughout much of the Siege, when I might have escaped, and by caring for the wounded, as I shall describe.

Happily, it was at this time that I found a new protector. (The Prince was of course much concerned with the progress of the war, and I saw him rarely; soon he was to leave Paris.) This was that same Baron Rogniat I had turned from my door a while ago, now somewhat more versed in polite society, and certainly cleaner than before. Caught in the middle of an unruly crowd on my way through a street near the Opéra – a friendly crowd, but one which disarranged me and even made me feel somewhat faint by its crush – I felt a hand on my arm and a male voice offered to escort me to safety. It was Rogniat, now engaged, it appeared, in dissipating a considerable fortune (having been reconciled with his family. He completed that process during the Siege; later, he re-made his fortune by starting a soap factory at Guita Vecchia.) I invited him back to the house to take tea. After tea, we played cards; after cards we had supper; after supper . . . He proved as energetic a lover as before, but rather more considerate. Though now almost forty, he had preserved the figure of a much younger man; he swam daily in the Seine throughout the year (a process more likely to damage than to preserve health, one would have thought), and this kept him fit, he said, and also resulted in his body being marvellously brown and tanned, and his arse especially, with its downy covering of black hair, one of the most expressive I have encountered. We got on famously now, our previous disagreement forgotten, and parted next morning with mutual expressions of pleasure and the intention of meeting again.

Pleasure of any kind was increasingly valuable in those days; by mid-September Paris was surrounded, the Prussian army having encircled the city to meet at Versailles, which had fallen without a single gesture of defiance. The Prussian Crown Prince, I am told, stood that day and looked over what seemed a vanquished city – but was not quite vanquished yet. There were grim scenes within, as deserters were marched through the streets, arms tied behind their backs to be shot as they deserved.

The situation may sound sufficiently exciting, but in fact boredom was the chief enemy; certainly I found life insufferably tedious, for all the men in Paris seemed too engaged in preparations for withstanding and breaking the Siege to have time for love, and social life was dead. It was not only I who found this; most of the people in the streets went about their business in tedium and with dull faces. There was a sensation at the end of September, however, when walking in the gardens I saw people staring and pointing upwards, and in the sky above the city I saw the celebrated airship *Neptune*, which had been found intact in a shed, repaired, and was making a flight outside the city above the heads of the Prussians. The success of that voyage was such that within the next few days four more airships took off and safely reached the world outside. It was then decided to send a prominent Minister out, to marshal resistance, and the Minister of the Interior, Léon Gambetta, was chosen.

By coincidence, I had been introduced to him only a few months before. His morals were such that he was the talk of my particular friends – though he frequented none of the salons where we commonly met, being addicted to coarser women. He was one of the ugliest men I have ever seen, with a matted coarse beard, largely grey though he was only in his early thirties, and with one eye almost protruding from its socket. He smelt abominably, and I have heard that his behaviour in the bedroom was loathsome in the extreme. However, his bravery on this occasion did much to outweigh these disadvantages. Having spent the previous night not in prayer but in a whorehouse, he appeared in the Place St-Pierre on the morning of October 3 in a fur coat prepared for him, we are told, by a group of his women, and climbed into his balloon, pale but resolute, and as it rose into the air out from its basket streamed a *tricolore*. Though fired on, and actually wounded in the hand, he reached safety (we later heard) to organize the war effort outside the city.

Never had I spent duller hours than now – relieved only by the occasional visit of Rogniat, who was never so tired by his exertions of the day (which I was never in fact able to discover the nature of) that he could not be revived by a little toying. One evening, to be sure, my friends Hurion and Brunet appeared, quite unannounced; both were now in uniform, Hurion having volunteered for the militia. Brunet was at a height of satisfaction, boasting of the number of boys he had had in one night (there being a large intake of young men into the forces); he appeared to have given up women altogether, and slept soundly on a couch at our side while Hurion and I celebrated our re-union, he reaching the apogee of pleasure no less than five times during the night. Boys, the latter explained, were all right when nothing else offered, but his natural bent was else-where – a fact that he made perfectly obvious!

It soon became clear that the most notable thing about Paris during the Siege was its lethargy. The theatre and opera were closed, and a curfew was imposed on the cafés, which all had to put up their shutters at ten o'clock, by which time the streets were so dark and empty that one might have been in some dull provincial town rather than the greatest capital city of Europe. We knew nothing of what was going on in the world outside, for although balloons were now leaving Paris regularly, none could come in. The result of this was that rumour spread like wildfire day upon day; one morning one would learn that a tunnel had been built to connect the centre of Paris with the provinces, and herds of sheep and cattle were being brought through it to sustain us through the winter; the next morning the Crown Prince of Prussia was dead and the Prussian army retreating; the next, any citizen of Paris could easily be smuggled out of the city by a secret route, provided he or she consented to be chloroformed in order not to betray it!

There were many newspapers on sale – a new one sprung up almost every day: *La Patrie en Danger*, *Le Combat*, *Le Reveil* . . . But since none of them had news to print, they equally were full of speculation and rumour; there was nothing in any of them that one had not heard before, a thousand times.

The weather soon offered another subject for discussion, for the winter was phenomenally cold. By December, fuel was so short that it was impossible to keep more than one room in the house even passably warm, and for the first time I was forced to make love, on the increasingly rare occasions when the opportunity offered itself, with a pile of bedclothes, coats and even curtains piled upon the bed. Coal-gas was rationed (for it was used to fill the envelopes of the escaping balloons), and oil was requisitioned. One morning, I woke to see a dark shape lying in the corner of my bedroom; when I examined it, it turned out to be a large and emaciated rat, which had doubtless broken in to find food, and had died of cold during the night. To have kept even that room warm would have needed at least a hundred kilograms of wood each day; the allowance for the whole house was seventy-five a week.

When we ventured out, it became clear that the city was being stripped of everything it was possible to burn: the streets were cleared of trees, and where one remained it was usually surrounded by a group of people tearing and hacking at it – even digging up the roots to find pieces of wood to take home for the fire. Even the churchyard trees were torn down, and when there was no more wood from these sources, crowds ranged the streets tearing down notices, fences, even the flimsier front doors of houses when they could do so.

We piled clothing upon ourselves until we bore no resemblance either to male or female, or even to human, shape. When, indoors, it was (rarely) warm enough to remove our outer clothing, we still resembled ill-tied parcels, for there was now no way of getting our clothes clean, and so we wore dark colours which did not look as dirty as they undoubtedly were. All the laundries were closed, and certainly we did not use our small amounts of fuel to heat water for cleaning clothes – or even, I fear, to clean ourselves. Men wore their shirts inside out when the insides became too dirty, and in the end I would have been ashamed to undress myself even before a lover – not only because of appearances, but for the dirt and stench, inimical to happy love making.

By now, perhaps happily, our blood too ran cold and thin, for everyone was hungry. The sheep and cattle brought into the city had vanished – milk and cheese were never to be seen, and there were now no vegetables. Horsemeat became a luxury, and soon people's pets began to vanish, and there was a kind of pride in confessing that one had enjoyed a slice of spaniel or of cat; next to horses, cats and dogs provided the most popular dishes. Rats were less popular, for they had to be served accompanied by highly-flavoured sauces if their flesh was to be palatable. The two great elephants, Castor and Pollux, at the *Jardin d'Acclimatation*, were killed, and I saw the latter's trunk hanging in the shop of Roos, at the Boucherie Anglais, priced at forty francs per pound. Camel flesh, and that of antelope, donkey, mule and wolf, was also to be bought, and reindeer was a brave luxury.

A kind of artificial bread, made, I believe, of wheat, rice and straw, came onto the market, together with artificial milk made of God knows what; candlegrease was mixed with cooking fat, and jam made of boiled horses' bones. I was able, prudently, to bulk out my ration at first with what I had stored, though I could have made a fortune by selling it on the black market, for by December, cheese, which at the beginning of the Siege had been two francs a pound, was fetching thirty francs, and potatoes, once F2.75 a bushel, were now F28.

When we were at the lowest point of misery, or so it seemed, worse befell; at the end of December the Prussians began shelling the city – began at Avron, to the east, which was soon evacuated; then the southern forts at Issy and Vanves, and finally, in January, Paris itself. The first shell fell in the Rue Lelande on the left bank, and another killed a little girl on her way home from school near the Luxembourg; the cemetery at Montparnasse was shelled, the bones of the dead being scattered to the light; one shell fell on a food queue, another on a bistro in the Rue l'Enfer.

Soon, three or four hundred shells were falling every day, and for four or five hours every night, especially around the Panthéon and the Invalides. When the hospital at Salpétrière was hit, I decided to turn my house in the Rue de Chaillot into a hospital (some of my friends did likewise, Blanche d'Antigny for one). Soon, as many as fifty wounded – some of them civilians, many of them soldiers – were laid there on mattresses in the rooms and corridors. All my sheets were brought out and used, some of them, alas, for shrouds, and many of my friends came to help nurse the men, led by a doctor whose fees I paid myself.

Many of the faces, and I expect the bodies, of the women who were nursing them were known to the injured, and this, with their gratitude, gave them the spirit to recover. It was astonishing to me to see how some of the less severely, but still painfully wounded men, perhaps with the lower part of a leg taken off, would have still the instinct to reach for a breast as its owner changed his dressing; truly, love is one of the most powerful of all human emotions. At first, I would be distressed to see some young fellow, weak from the effects of a still scarce healed wound, squander his energies (as I thought) in attempting to make love to his nurse. But the doctor assured me that no man had been found to die of making love, and that in his opinion it offered them the hope of life, and that the pleasure seemed positively to give strength. Upon which I encouraged the girls to give of themselves freely, while taking care to save the wounded from making movements which might unnecessarily strain them or affect their wounds. No ill effects were ever observed by me, nor did I hear anything beyond expressions of the keenest gratitude from the men. This may perhaps profitably be made known to nurses in more conventional hospitals, where care is commonly taken to avoid that human contact between nurse and patient which might give rise to carnal enjoyment, though the latter can, I am convinced, contribute to the profitable and speedy recovery of health.

I was myself so tired at this time that I failed for the first time in my life to rouse interest in love making, and rejected several offers of companionship made to me by officers visiting the hospital on behalf of their men, or to make enquiries about them. Rogniat continued to come to me from time to time, but was now so considerate that he would be content to lie with me in his arms without demanding anything other than that I should allow him to bring himself off while I lay half asleep under him. My appreciation of our plight was made more acute when Rogniat, one evening throwing off his clothes before me (the room for once being warm with a fire from some wood brought by the grateful father of a wounded officer) disclosed a body wasted by want of food so that it seemed no more than skin and bones, his once fine arse now resembling more a pair of ancient bellows.

I now received a visit from an official at the British Embassy. I thought, in my simpleness, that he had perhaps been instructed to give some recognition of the work a countrywoman was doing for her adopted country. An upright young man dressed in a manner which suggested that few of the privations of the Parisians were shared by the British at the embassy, he stood in the hallway, handkerchief to his nose, looking distastefully at the bodies lying there waiting to be taken away for burial. (Commonly we lost one or two men every night, to death.) I showed him into the small cloakroom which was my office, whereupon he said to me that attention had been drawn by a visiting Englishman (it was still possible for such to enter Paris) to the fact that I was flying the Cross of St George above the house, and that it was the opinion at the embassy that it was improper for the national flag of England to be flying above a house which had formerly been known to be the gathering place for men and women of loose morals. I would please see that it was removed.

I have never been so angry. With a strength I did not know I possessed, I seized the young man by his well-laundered collar, marched him from the house and over to the other side of the street, where the red cross could be seen flying. If he did not know the symbol of pity and care from the British flag, I said, it was time he returned to school – if indeed he had ever attended one. I then, I am sorry to say – no, that is a lie; I am delighted to say – delivered a kick in a region which I suspected he had little use for, and squeaking with pain he hobbled off. That was the only recognition I was to receive from anyone for the attempts I made to care for the wounded.[1]

Perhaps it was this incident, and my consequent irritation, which began to give me thoughts of leaving the city if I could. My chance was to come almost before the thought of it, for within a week Brunet and Hurion called on me in some distress. They had been ordered to leave Paris by balloon the following week, with dispatches for the forces outside the city. I could see that Hurion was excited by the prospect, but Brunet was far from so; he had, it seems, fallen desperately in love with a young lad in his regiment, and was reluctant to leave him – indeed, the two were thinking of deserting, in order to live together.

[1] But several obituaries of Cora Pearl, on her death, recalled her bravery and the services she performed during the Siege.

An idea occurred to me, and I was quick to express it. I was somewhat of Brunet's build. If I took his place in the balloon, suspicion would be lulled long enough for him to disappear; and as for the army outside Paris – how were they to know that more than Hurion were ordered to leave the city? So it was that in ten days' time, the two men came to my house early one morning. Brunet quickly stripped, dressing himself in an old suit which he had brought with him, and crept away with thanks to me, while I put on his uniform, having cropped my hair and bound my breasts with a scarf. Even so, it was difficult enough for me to get into his breeches and tunic; after some efforts I managed it – but not before Hurion was getting impatient. We left the house, myself taking only a small case containing money and jewels, and Hurion with the dispatch case containing papers for the outside world.

At the Place St Pierre we found the balloon half inflated, and soon were into the basket, the dim light of torches showing the faces of the men holding on to it. A further hiss of gas, the further inflation of the envelope, an uneasy stirring and a sudden sensation, not unpleasant, indicated that we had left the soil of Paris. Soon the glow of the torches had vanished, and we were in complete darkness (there was no moon) and almost complete silence, except for the strange sound of voices far below.

We drifted for what seemed like days without any reference to the world, without any sign that anyone else but us existed. We huddled for warmth beneath Hurion's cloak, and the minutes passed interminably, one after the other, until dawn revealed open country beneath us, and no sign of the Prussian army. At last we saw the tents of an assembly of soldiers, and Hurion pulled a rope which let gas out of the envelope. We came to earth at about half past eight in the morning near Gués-des-Grues, eight kilometres from Dreux. The army camp was barely half a kilometre away, where at first they treated us with great suspicion, for spies had been known to descend from balloons, pretending to be refugees from Paris. But the documents Hurion produced soon satisfied the commanding officer, and we were taken to a tent where there was a huge tub of hot water, and left to bathe ourselves – for it was all too well known that those who had been for hours in the upper atmosphere were generally chilled to the bone, quite apart from the ingrained dirt of all refugees from the capital (who were sometimes, indeed, verminous).

By dint of remaining silent and standing at what passed for a soldierly attention, I had concealed the fact that I was not a man; for it was somewhat a puzzle as to how to reveal it. It did not occur to me for the moment that I was a female, so welcome was the sight of the tub. In a moment we had thrust off our uniforms and were into the water, soaping ourselves and revelling in the cleanliness of our limbs. The feeling of freedom began to make its effect, and the exhilaration of success soon showed itself in Hurion's spirits rising; he began to caress me with an impatience less directed at washing than at rousing. I was nothing loath, and taking the soap lathered his manhood and smoothed it until it stood ironhard, the crest rising blood-red out of a mound of white bubbles! Then, as he sat upon his heels in the huge tub, the water about his waist, I lowered myself upon him until we were thoroughly joined, and rode him with increasing fervour until the water slapped and splashed and slopped over the side of the tub, and our wet bodies coming together applauded our efforts with their own clapping.

As we were in the midst of our play, I heard an exclamation behind me, and turning my head saw the commanding officer, who had entered the tent unannounced (as well he might, its occupants being, as he believed, two serving soldiers). He may have suspected Hurion of being a Brunet at first, for my back was to him, but just as Hurion reached his ecstacy, I drew myself away and turned, so that there could have been no doubt as to my sex, my body being almost completely disclosed. The officer's jaw dropped yet further; but eventually he collected himself, saluted, and said with a fair display of courtesy that he had not realized that Hurion had brought with him something even more valuable than the papers. I realized that he had recognized me, and indeed it turned out that he had been a visitor at the Château several years previously; he had heard from other refugees of my work for the wounded, and quite accepted our explanation that the commander of Hurion's regiment had acceded to my request that I should leave Paris that way, being too familiar to the enemy to be permitted egress as a British citizen. This was fortunate for Hurion, who otherwise might have found himself in trouble.

We lunched with Commandant Ponciez, and then I was given a tent to myself in which to rest while he and Hurion went through the dispatches together. I woke from a deep sleep to find the Commandant at the door of my tent enquiring after my health. He asked if he could pay his respects, by which he meant something warmer than a kiss of the hand, and I invited him to do so. The tent was marvellously warm, being heated by several lamps; and the comfort, after the cold of the city, warmed my spirits wonderfully. The Commandant was not unmoved to see me naked, and paid a compliment to my looks, though he regretted I had had to remove my hair; 'but, madame,' he added, 'there can after all be no doubt of your femininity. Is there anyone with more womanly qualities than Madame Cora Pearl?'

The effects of months of deprivation of comfortable loving made me ready to acknowledge his affection, and he was an attractive man, though of middle age; and as it turned out he was as self-controlled in love-making as no doubt in commanding his troops, so he was able to give me sufficient pleasure to compensate me for the time of my denial. We were interrupted only by his servant, who appeared with a bottle of fine champagne (coming in without announcing himself, he placed the bottle and glasses at our side, the Commandant not for a moment losing the rhythm of his movements, nor being disconcerted at presenting his servant with a view of his naked and active arse as he worked above me).

We lay together that night, and after renewed thanks and a farewell to Hurion, who was now returned to duty, I left for England.

CHAPTER NINE

London – dull days – the Gaiety Theatre – a young admirer –
the Café Royal – the innocent experienced – a fortunate
person – Lady Greber – Vigor's Horse-Action Saddle –
batheing dress – advantageous to gentlemen – men repugnant
to Mrs Rundall – Mr Rundall introduced – conversation in
the bathroom – an interesting reconciliation – return to Paris

I took the precaution, supposing London to be full of
refugees from France (which turned out not to be the case)
of telegraphing to the manager of the Grosvenor Hôtel,
near Victoria Station, reserving in advance a suite on the
first floor for which I paid three months' rent in advance.
However, when I had stayed there only two days a knock
on the door of my rooms announced the manager, who
asking me if I was Mademoiselle Cora Pearl and, receiving
an affirmative, told me that I could not be allowed to stay
at the hotel, and that moreover none of my money could be
returned! It was clear that someone had been spreading
scandal, and that in England the middle-class attitudes
which resulted in the prosperity of an enormous under-
growth of crime and vice was still in operation!

Happily, I was able to contact Prince Napoléon, who
made enquiries at several more hôtels but in the end
rejected them all because of the large number of Germans
staying there, and took for me a large house on Campden
Hill, a pleasant rural spot somewhat to the west of
Kensington Gardens, for which he paid one thousand
pounds for five weeks. The house was splendidly furnished,

and the bedroom in particular was a great deal more luxurious than English bedrooms usually are. The Prince also went to the Grosvenor Hôtel, addressed the manager with particular sternness, and succeeded in recovering for me most of the money I had paid him. But the Prince was now melancholy and short of temper, appearing to have nothing to do, and spending his time wandering about London seeking out refugees from Paris and attempting to find out what had happened to his old colleagues and friends. He was in fact never to be himself again, and although briefly allowed to revisit Paris after the raising of the Siege, was shortly banned again, and is now an international wanderer living sometimes in Milan, sometimes in Switzerland, sometimes in London. Even on that first day of our re-meeting, having taken me to temporary rooms in Lancaster Gate, he left me almost immediately, and I did not sleep with him once while I was in the city.

It was strange to find myself in London again. I went about the city to look at some of the old places I so well remembered, but many of them were sadly altered or closed down, or even did not exist any more, and the city seemed dull and lifeless when I compared it to the Paris of even a year ago – although blessedly quiet after the Paris of the bombardment. News from France was of nothing but the distress of the population, and I thought with pity and horror of my friends still there as I sat down to splendid meals in the evenings at very little cost. For the most part I was alone, and the men whom I did meet, or with whom I exchanged glances in public, seemed to be less adventurous than in my old days at the Argyll Rooms.

I had, however, one engaging adventure. At the Gaiety Theatre, a very pleasant house which had only been open for two or three years, at the far end of the Strand, I sat one evening next to a handsome, dark-haired youth obviously much younger than he pretended to be. He affected the manners of a man-about-town, but his pleasure in the spectacle was such that he was obviously at a theatre for the first time. He paid especial attention to the girls, who wore skimpy clothing (though not as provocative as those of many actresses in Paris), and to my astonishment as we watched one item on the programme with the lights low, I felt his hand fall upon the top of my thigh and press it. I was not equally surprised to find myself responding, for it was not three weeks since I had left Hurion in France, and the Prince had left me very much alone since my arrival. I therefore pressed my leg against the young admirer's, and after a moment allowed my hand to rest on his.

When the lights went up, he lost no time in asking me to dine with him. He was a slim lad, with no vestige of beard and only the faint traces of a moustache, with dark and sparkling eyes and a ready smile. I was happy to accept his invitation, and at the end of the performance we met at the theatre doors and he hailed a cab and directed it to the Café Royal. There we ate a good meal and drank a bottle or two of wine, though I was disappointed that we had not a private room, and set it down to the inexperience – or perhaps the lack of money – in the boy. He talked readily of London and Paris, though without I think any real knowledge of either city, and was interested to hear that I had lately been in the Siege. It turned out that he intended to leave shortly for America, though he ventured no information about his family or circumstances. Towards the end of the meal he grew thoughtful, and after a while said:

'Madame Pearl, I would much like to invite you to take wine with me in my rooms; but to be honest, I am staying with relatives, and my rooms are not my own. During the next two evenings I must take my leave of my various relations and friends, and I am loath to leave you discourteously at the table.'

By now I would have been equally sorry, and almost without a thought I said that if he cared to, he could take a glass of wine at my house. His eyes brightened as he agreed, and in a moment we were in a cab and on our way to Campden Hill. As we jogged through the streets he leaned over and kissed me on the lips for the first time, and I felt a lively little tongue probing as his hand slid down the front of my dress to fondle a breast. I drew back after a while with a gasp; a moment more and we would have been drawn into exertions greater than the interior of a cab would provide safety for!

At Campden Hill he paid off the cab, and I led him without preamble to the bedroom on the first floor, where before I had the candles lit he had stripped himself naked and thrown himself on the bed! I joined him soon enough, expecting an immediate onslaught from so young a lover (and, to be honest, too speedy a conclusion); but to my surprise he simply raised himself on one elbow and looked at me, stroking my body with a hand that seemed almost to tremble, and occasionally leaning to imprint a kiss on a breasts, on my navel, on the top of my thigh, and eventually on the bush. Indeed, it was clear that though his excitement was great, he was capable of containing it, and this excited me almost past bearing; but I would have been ashamed to show more impatience than a boy – for his body was thin and 'gawky' as we used to say in Plymouth in my childhood; the hands were big and the wrists awkward. But it was a beautiful body nevertheless, with a full chest tapering away to a narrow waist, a body hairless except for a clutch of hair around the eager tool, which itself seemed the only part of his body to counterfeit adulthood, as it throbbed with every heartbeat, a bright pink head appearing through the fold of white skin at the tip.

At last, I leaned over and took his tool between my lips, at which he breathed 'O! you darling!' and I felt his whole body quiver with excitement so that I dared continue only for a moment lest he should not contain himself. As I turned once more on to my back and opened my thighs to receive him, he said: 'The first time!' – which I took to mean that no woman had kissed him in that way before. Lying between my thighs, he wriggled down so that he could kiss me in a similar manner, and with a natural expertise, not only his tongue but his lips themselves and even his chin combining to raise me speedily to his own pitch of excitement, so that I was forced to take his head between my hands and raise it from me so that I could look into his eyes as my body tensed in its rapture. I lay panting, and he smiled at me, then slid his body up along mine until he could enter me, beginning then a movement which was not rash as a young man's movements so often are, but slow and rhythmic and free, without anxiety and without haste, carrying me away so that my excitement once more mounted.

I might have been the innocent, and he the whore, so wonderfully did he control his love making, until after what seemed an age I felt his muscles tighten and tense, as his buttocks clenched and he made the final thrust and I felt his essence hot within me. We lay bound together by our perspiration for an age, until eventually he raised himself – not merely rolling away as most men do – and lifted himself on to his side, resting his head in the crook of my arm, and touching with his tongue the beads of perspiration on my skin there.

I complimented him on his skill, and asked his name. He was eager now to talk, and told me his name was Frank, that he was fifteen years old – and moreover that this was his first experience of the full joys of love. It astonished me; but clearly he was one of those fortunate beings naturally predisposed to love, and indeed when I questioned him he confessed that from the age even of four or five, when he used to crawl beneath a table to examine the legs of the girls sitting around it, he had been fixed upon thoughts of women, though while at school he had curbed his natural ardour for the sake of his interest in sport (how English!), and that only in the holidays had he allowed himself to approach girls. But he had so far been unlucky in finding one who would allow him full possession, though he spoke happily of one in particular, Ethel or Edith, who when he was thirteen had allowed him, at the rehearsals of a choir to which they both belonged, to play with her person beneath her clothes while they sang! But (again, how English!) neither she nor the other girls who permitted him certain liberties, would allow him further. How much they lost by this! – for he was certainly the most talented lover of his age I ever experienced, and needed none of the schooling which, for instance, I had had to bestow on the young peasant Marcel, at Beauséjour.[1]

Frank allowed that he was indeed more interested in love than in anything else in life other than literature, for his mind also seemed fixed on books; he was going to America in the hopes that a new country and new challenges would enable him to use his energies more positively. 'For,' he said, 'I must make money if I am to make my way.'

After a while first he, then I, drifted into sleep; again at one point of the night he woke me by tickling my thighs gently with his fingers, and this time he slipped into me easily and rode me for a brief time almost without passion,

---

[1] The facts given accord with those given by Frank Harris in his autobiography *My Life and Loves*, but that nothing is said there of his visiting London before leaving for America, nor is such an episode recorded. The coincidence is interesting, but it is surely impossible that Harris, in such a frank record of his sexual adventures, should have omitted this one – especially if it was his initiation.

like an affectionate brother rather than a lover. I woke with the first light, and looked at him as he lay, the clothes thrown back, his head on the pillow with dark curls, one hand on his breast and the other resting on his thigh, its fingers brushing his tool, now small but beautifully shaped and tapering, the skin at its tip relaxed and drawn into a tiny spout. I leaned to examine it, its softness, the way its slim trunk vanished into the curls at its base – I had forgotten what a really young man's – a boy's – body was like. At last, I lowered my head and took it between my lips, softly mumbling it; at first it swelled only slightly, then of a sudden began to grow until it felt like warm marble as I moved my lips over it, finally with a series of tiny jerks reaching full stature, and I felt his hand on my head, softly caressing the back of it, and drew away to look into his eyes, still slow with sleep, but enlivening with growing desire.

This time he drew me from the bed to the thick carpet before my tall mirror, which he tilted, and then mounted me from behind, so that he could watch us in the mirror as he butted me, his belly smacking against my rump, and his neat little arse looking so puny! He stroked my back, running his thumbs down each side of my spine, then leaned and toyed with my breasts, taking each nipple between finger and thumb, then slipped his hand down to my belly and finally played about me as he continued to plough, so exciting me that when we came together it was as intense a moment of pleasure as I have experienced, and breathless we collapsed laughing and gasping on to the rugs. Presently he leaned over to kiss me where the juices still dripped. We dressed in silence.

With only small encouragement, I would have begged him to stay; I felt, although it is wicked to say so, as though he might be both son and lover to me. But he was to be neither, for in a few minutes he was gone, and I knew only his Christian name – Frank. I have never seen him since.

Forced to entertain myself, I decided to seek out the possibility of some hunting, so much of my pleasure in France having been in the field, and my never having ridden in England. I mentioned this to Lady Greber, a neighbour in Campden Hill, of impeccable virtue and great plainness, but of robust health. To my surprise, she said to me that I need stir no more than a hundred yards from home, and that if I presented myself at her home at ten on the following morning, properly attired, I should have a good ride. At that time I left my house and walked the few steps to her door, and was taken to a room at the back of the house where foxes' masks hung on the wall, and where in the middle of the floor stood a strange looking machine, square on four legs, with a sort of handle at the front, and a leather saddle upon it.

Lady Greber explained that this was Vigor's Horse-Action Saddle, as used by the Princess of Wales. She climbed upon it, and set it in motion, whereupon it mechanically performed the actions of the trot, canter and gallop, as explained in the brochure which was shown me, remarking that it 'invigorated the system by bringing all the vital organs into inspiriting action; a complete cure for obesity, hysteria and gout.'

I was not greatly persuaded by this, and explained to Lady Greber that what I had in mind was similar activity but performed in society, whereupon she kindly gave me an introduction to friends of hers, Mr and Mrs Edward Rundall, of Brighton, both being much associated with the Southdown Foxhounds. Having got into touch with them, they kindly invited me for the weekend, to bathe and to ride.

Sea-batheing was something I had no experience of,

though I swam regularly as possible in the river at Beauséjour. I had brought no batheing costume with me (indeed,
possessed none, there being no necessity at home); Mrs
Rundall, or Sarah, as she asked me to call her, took me to a
shop where I could buy one, and offered to advise me. She
was herself a tall, statuesque figure, handsome rather than
pretty, and explained that her own batheing dress was
similar to the first shown me – of navy serge, a heavy and
unglamorous material most suitable for maids. It was cut
square at the neck, high above the bosom, and its white
trimmings and pearl buttons did nothing to make it more
acceptable.

I demurred, but Sarah insisted that I should try it on,
and accompanied me into the small room, with mirrors,
which the shop set aside for such a purpose. When I
undressed, Sarah exclaimed at my beauty, and was eager in
helping me to climb into the strange garment, which had
knickerbockers below the knee and a very full skirt over
them. Surely, I said, this must be very unpleasant when
wet? and Sarah agreed that indeed it tended to sag and fill,
sometimes slipping off the shoulders altogether, as she had
once seen happen to a friend, who being small breasted was
revealed naked to the waist before her friends. 'But that
could never happen to you,' said Sarah, placing her hand
upon my breast with a gesture of affection which seemed
warmer than entirely necessary.

Indeed it was clear to me by the eagerness with which she
helped to slip the costume over my hips that her husband,
nor no man, possessed only a small part of her affections
[sic]; she was all eyes, and even went so far as to slip her hand
beneath the costume to smooth it over my thighs. She soon
had me in another costume, rather more agreeable, again in
serge, but this time black with white trimmings rather than
the dark blue of the former, also with narrow black braid,

the knickerbockers and bodice cut in one (no doubt a factor for safety when such a heavy cloth was wet!) and with a skirt buttoning over, and short puff sleeves. It was clear to me that no batheing dress was to have the advantages of my normal wear for swimming, so I bought this.

Next day I was taken to the beach and escorted to a batheing machine – a square hut on wheels – in which Sarah and I put on our 'costumes'. Sarah explained that this was a recent fashion only, for even now on many beaches outside the centre of the town men and women bathed naked, but at Brighton there had been complaints from ladies of seeing naked men emerging from the sea, and the authorities had enforced the wearing of swimming clothes. This had the effect that many ladies wore dresses of thin material which when wet clung to the figure so closely that no secret was to be kept; and since the gentlemen, now both sexes were clothed, felt it no longer necessary to keep a distance, they were afforded a close view of the shape of a breast and an extended nipple, and of every curve of the body – much more so than when both had been unclothed, and a polite distance had been observed.

We leaped straight from the door of the machine into the sea, which was rough and cold, so that when we retired again even after a short period my skin was covered with pimples and I was shivering; we threw off our costumes, and Sarah insisted on rubbing me all over with a rough towel, with such attention and vigour that I wondered whether the whole thing had not been planned, for she paid especial attention to my breasts, buttocks and female parts. She then invited me to 'warm her', which being her guest, I did; she was of a sturdy and muscular build, with breasts which were firm rather than full, indeed no more presenting the chest of a woman than of some men I have known.

We dined alone that night. I had been puzzled not to

find Mr Rundall at home when I arrived, but it had been explained to me that he had been away on business, and would return the following morning. The supper lacked nothing which might have been served to him, however, including a very full supply of wine and spirits. We said goodnight and retired – but I had scarcely settled into my bed when the door opened and Sarah appeared, clad in a voluminous gown, 'to see if I was comfortable'. I wore, as is my habit when alone, a simple silk night-gown, which she affected to admire, drawing the bedclothes back the better to see it, and stroking the material where it lay over my hips and side.

It soon transpired that she wished to share my bed, at first because, she said, she did not like to be alone; but then, as I showed no sign of accepting that explanation, she told me quite frankly that not long after her marriage she discovered that men and their figures were if not entirely repugnant at least unexciting to her, whereas an admiration for the female figure was what she could not but give vent to. Since my adventure with Frank, I had lived the life of a nun, and although I had not a natural feeling for female company in bed, I was ready for a physical comfort, and accepted Sarah's advances, which soon began to return to me memories of my nights in the dormitory in Boulogne, and which proved far from repugnant. Though it is true that almost every male lover has, even after some tuition, been able to give me some pleasure, it is also a fact that another woman must more securely know, through pleasuring herself, how to pleasure a fellow of her sex, and Sarah was certainly an exampler. I cannot promise that I was as happy in her arms as in those of almost any of my male lovers; but neither can I deny that I enjoyed her attentions, and from her gasps, moans and mewings, which at times I feared would rouse the house, she enjoyed mine.

At dawn, Sarah left me, and I dozed for an hour before rising. I had been shown a bathroom just along the corridor, and at eight o'clock left my bedroom and made my way there. I heard a splashing of water, and took this as evidence that the maid who was caring for me had obeyed my instructions to draw me a bath at that hour; so opening the door, I stepped in, closing it behind me – only looking up to see a man, stark naked and covered with soap-bubbles, standing in the bath-tub. He was a fair, handsome fellow, a typical Englishman, with a little moustache, a broad chest, and a manhood which, perhaps stimulated by a thorough soaping, was larger than many I had seen even in a fully excited state. We looked at each other a for a moment, but then with the utmost coolness he said 'Madame Pearl, I believe?' and extended his hand.

Coolness of that sort is what I admire, and I stepped forward, touched his hand with mine, and dropped him a curtsy.

'I must apologize,' I said, 'but I had instructed the maid to draw me a bath, and . . .'

'Think nothing of it!' he replied; 'I should have remembered that this is the room you would use. I shall not be long. Please be free to stay and talk – for, if you will forgive me, I cannot believe that you are not familiar with the male body, or that you will be embarrased if I continue my ablutions!' And he gave a smile which robbed his words of any possible offence.

So I sat on the chair which held his towels, and he sat and began to rub his shoulders and arms with the bath-cloth. He was looking forward to riding with me tomorrow, he said; had I found Brighton interesting? Had I seen much of the town? Batheing was something he was not fond of, but Sarah enjoyed it. I said that I had bathed the previous day, but that the sea had been cold enough to dissuade me from doing so again; however, Sarah had succeeded in warming me afterwards – at which I thought he looked somewhat taken aback, but since he obviously knew all about me, I said right out that I had been deprived of masculine company for some weeks, and that personal contacts were important to me.

'Then you do not object to – eh –'

'Not at all,' I said; 'Sarah has been very kind, and I hope I have rewarded her kindness.'

At which he rose to his feet, his skin glistening, and I passed him a towel, which he passed over himself rapidly, not troubling to disguise the fact that his tool had now risen to truly splendid proportions.

'If I am not over-importunate,' he said, 'perhaps I might offer you my own hospitality, as compensation for anything you may have lacked in Sarah's attentions?'

Merely clasping the towel about his waist, he accompanied me back to my bedroom, where he soon proved to me that the head of the household was no less impervious to female charms than its distaff; as he supported himself on his hands, my legs thrown over his shoulders, but otherwise his tool the only contact between us, the door of the bedroom opened and the maid appeared. Catching my eye, she simply bobbed, and said that she was about to draw my bath – then retired without the faintest sign of embarrassment. Mr Rundall, having reached the heights, explained as he completed drying his body, still damp from the bath, that the maid was unlikely to be surprised at anything she saw in the house in the way of love making; and it was clear that the Rundalls' servants were trained much as my own – to see all but say nothing; nor did either master or mistress have any connection with them, since a young footman had misinterpreted Sarah's habit of negligently appearing naked in his presence as a sign of infatuation rather than of the indifference it really was, and had attempted her; she, thinking perhaps (it was early in their marriage) that another man might please her more than Mr Rundall (an unlikely probability, my single experience of his attentions suggested!) allowed him the liberty, whereupon he had attempted to obtain money by the threat of telling her husband. He, when she informed him, had taken his revenge by forcing the footman to strip himself, and then taking him in his carriage to the centre of town and tipping him out to take his chance there.

The day was a pleasant one, which we spent in leisure. Sarah learned from her husband that we had introduced ourselves, and showed no jealousy; to be brief, it was clear that husband and wife took their pleasure where they found it, and if it was found in the same place, that was no bar to their enjoyment. So it was that we ended the day in the same bed, where our revels continued for some hours, entirely satisfactory to us all. Though I had many times sported with two men in my bed, and occasionally in the way of business had consented to frolic with another woman for the gratification of a lover, this was the first occasion on which pleasure was the only motive, and pleasure indeed it was, both Mr and Mrs Rundall paying me flattering and continual attention, and even, when we had exhausted all combinations, lying together, while I by manipulating his stones and at the same time attending to Sarah's most sensitive part, gave them the simultaneous thrill they never experienced together under other circumstances. The tenderness with which they embraced each other after spending convinced me that they were truly a loving couple, and that nature had played them a cruel trick in denying them the natural instincts through which they could please each other as lovers ought.

Next morning, though tired after our exertions, we rose

early and rode to Ditchling, beyond the downs, there to join the Southdown hounds for a good day out. It was a sorrow that I boarded the train that evening, with many protestations of affection to my host and hostess, and invitations on my part for them to visit me in France when I had returned.

When the tenancy of my house expired, the Prince invited me to accompany him to Switzerland, which I did, never having seen that country. It proved a sad disappointment, the splendour of the scenery palling very soon, the Prince proving as melancholy and neglectful as he had been in London, and the Swiss men being lacking in attention to me, or as far as I could see to their own women. After a week, I insisted that I must return to Paris; the Prince attempted to dissuade me, but on my proving adamant, arranged for me to share the carriage of a French diplomat riding from Geneva to Paris. My heart rose at the prospect, and even the fact that the diplomat proved to be a man of seventy whose attentions were exclusively upon the buttocks of the outriders, did not lower my spirits. In February of 1871, then, I rode into Paris in the midst of a convoy taking food to the starving citizens. I did not think it wrong to take a large ham, some concentrated milk, some herrings, jam and Apps' cocoa offered me by the escorting officer, who knew me from the previous years. At my house I found nothing but empty rooms – empty of people, that is, for there had been little pilfering or sacking, and my furniture was for the most part intact. A watch must have been kept on the house, for within twenty-four hours four servants returned, my maid showing me where, in an attic, she had concealed the jewellery I had not taken with me on my travels. Soon, the house was running as smoothly as ever, and having restored order there I began to look about me.

CHAPTER TEN

*Paris not itself – the Prussians leave – violence in the streets –
the Commune – Brunet reappears – death – the end of the
Commune – Duval and the Bouillons – Rue de Chaillot –
return to normal – Duval importunate – Hurion returns –
Duval attempts suicide – plots against me – London – Nice*

If I had hoped that with the end of the war Paris might be
restored to its true self, I had to think again; even
compared to the dullness of London, the city was still
unfamiliar – partly because it was occupied by the Prussians, partly because it was badly scarred, the trees all cut
down, the wreckage from the bombardment spilling across
many of the streets, and the long starvation which had
affected almost everyone had made people so enervated
that even their hatred of the Prussians was muted; indeed
such energy as they still possessed was devoted to finding
food. People still mistrusted each other, too – saw spies
under every bed, suspected any woman who appeared well
nourished of conducting affairs with the Prussians, and
thus becoming a sympathizer with the enemy.

The result of the elections which were held added to the
difficulties, for the conservative candidates swept the board
– comforting many of my friends, but infuriating the
ordinary Parisians, who believed themselves betrayed by
the Frenchmen in the country, who had not suffered as
they had.

Things became more cheerful in March, when the Prussians marched away. Bonfires were lit in the streets to burn

any piece of equipment or clothing they left behind, the houses where they had stayed were fumigated or even burned down, and many people went so far as to scrub the pavements outside their houses with disinfectant to remove even the slightest trace of Prussian footprints. Soon, the street-lights were lit again, spring began to lighten the evening skies, and things began to look as though they were returning to normal. My first hint that this might be the case occurred when a few of my friends came to call, and my evenings once more were filled with talk; my bed was relatively quiet, however – for the men who called were thin and lacking in vigour because of the long struggle, and love seemed to be far from their minds.

There was of course still much trouble. At the end of February I saw crowds making their way to the left-wing demonstration on behalf of the National Guard, which rumour said was to be disbanded. A poor man seen noting down parts of a speech made before the crowd at the foot of the July column was cried as a spy, thrown into the Seine, and when he refused to sink was stoned until his body fell apart. Beatings, stonings, the arrest of innocent passers-by happened daily, and although women were not often the subject of such incidents I judged it best to remain as much as possible indoors, alone and bored, and when the Commune was declared I was even less inclined to show myself, despite the lovely spring weather. (The spring of that year was one of the loveliest in my memory, a dreadful backcloth to the terror in the streets.)

As April and May passed, the number of people arrested, killed, beaten – the number of people who, like the Archbishop of Paris himself, simply vanished into the prisons never to be seen again – increased daily. I continued to keep to the house, and saw no-one; I even took care not to show myself at the windows, for fear that someone would take it into their head to break into the house and arrest us all. Rogniat seemed to have left the city, and no-one offered himself as a positive protector.

One night late in May I woke in the early morning to a rattle of stones at my window; for a time I simply stayed in bed, then as the rattling continued, and there was a whispered call of my name, I cautiously put out my head. Two shadowy figures stood below, and one identified himself as Brunet. I let him in, and with him a slim boy with huge dark eyes, as wasted and emaciated in body (when they had removed their greatcoats) as Brunet himself – the boy for whom he had deserted as I left Paris. Since then, Brunet explained, he and his lover, Pierrot, had lived more or less in hiding, surviving the months of the Siege in the cellar of an old flour mill in Montmartre; but now the area in which they had taken refuge was a hot-bed of the Commune, and the previous night they had been warned by the owner of the mill that it was to be taken over by Raoul Rignault, the police chief of Paris, a dirty and amoral brute who had sentenced many priests to death, and whose attitude to two male lovers would, in view of his own womanising, have been entirely without pity.

Naturally, I allowed the two men to stay, gave them a room in the attics, allowed them to bathe, and fed them. The boy was pitifully grateful; he was a sensitive, charming lad who had grown up near Chartres, and would have been much more at home on a farm than in the heart of a city, but having been taken for the Army had grieved and longed for escape until that escape was made possible by Brunet falling in love with him. Their mutual love was indeed wonderully apparent.

After a few days in what was for them luxury (they spent much of the day with me, and I heard of their privations, which had, among other things – so Brunet said – strengthened the spiritual bond between them, since malnutrition and dirt and danger had removed from them any desire for carnal connection) they recovered their spirits, and Brunet and I were happy to recall some of the stories of former days and ways, amusing Pierrot with them, who of course was completely ignorant of the style of life we used to live. It was good to see how the two lovers recovered their physical affection for each other, as adequate food brought back strength to their bodies. Once, I was so lonely in my own bed – unvisited by a single lover for so long – that I summond them to keep me company, and the three of us clung, naked, together for comfort. Brunet was as handsome as ever, though still thin, and I could not help wishing that he would make love to me as he used to when our mutual friend Hurion was there to help. Pierrot was equally handsome, or I might even say 'beautiful', for he had a feminine sensibility, and his body was of such youthful perfection that I could not wonder at his command of Brunet's love. Their gratitude to me was such that, relying on Pierrot's caresses to support him, Brunet was able to mount me and bring me to an almost satisfactory peak before, his eye falling on his lover's body, with an apology he slipped from my arms to Pierrot's; as I watched them, their bodies moving as they rubbed their bellies together to their acute satisfaction, I was forced to bring myself off, though in tears at my own lack of a lover.

Two days later, looking out of the window into the deserted street, and bemoaning the fact that our stock of food had fallen so low that we were reduced to very meagre rations, we saw the body of a man lying not far from the front door, still clutching a side of beef. Despite our fears, young Pierrot must go out to take it for us. We watched as he ran from the house, bent over the body, straightened up with the meat in his arms. He turned, and looked up for a moment at us, a broad smile on his face. Then a shot rang out, and a second later Pierrot's face appeared to turn to a red mask before he fell to the ground. Brunet, leaning over my shoulder, made an inarticulate noise in his throat, and then ran to the door, down the stairs, out of the front door. He raised Pierrot to his feet, clasping him to his breast like a lover; then another shot was heard, and the two men whirled for a moment like dancers before collapsing, Brunet with his face thrust into Pierrot's chest, while the latter's head, twisted on one side, fell onto an outstretched arm. I threw the shutters closed. By next morning, the bodies had gone.

Now, I could not regret that male company no longer exercised me; it was scarcely the time for loving, however boring the days were. I would have been pleased with any protection when, in May, the Commune died in a welter of blood and fire. My house was happily untouched, though we had collected as much water as we could in pails and baths, in case some incendiary set fire to the lower rooms; the houses on the opposite side of the street were burned to the ground, but the wind was in the right quarter to spare us, and even the immense heat did only the damage of cracking some of the window panes. Of the many hundreds of executions I saw nothing, other than one man shot down in the street by the army, taking him for an incendiary because of his blackened hands. Whether he was, or no, I cannot say. It is said that twenty thousand people perished during the Commune and after, from the excesses on one side and then upon the other; I know of no friends who died other than Brunet and poor Pierrot, but there were several both men and women I never saw again, and who may have fallen victim to the natural result of too keen an interest in the times.

When the town was again quiet, I looked about me and

found that for the first time for many years I was in need of money. I had my house, and the Château was undamaged (though it was as yet unsafe to travel there); I had jewels, and could have sold them – except that jewels were now the commonest currency, and prices were low. Of money I had virtually none, having spent most of my coin on turning my house into a hospital (for little thanks). From this position I was rescued by one man – Alexander Duval.

M. Duval was a man in his late twenties, the son of a butcher from Les Halles, who in the 1860s had started a chain of restaurants with the slogan *bouillons et boeuf*. These were scarcely the establishments which my admirers brought me to before the war, but the *bourgeoisie* attended them in vast numbers. At the Bouillons Duval, the first and best known of which was at the corner of the Rue Tronchet and the Rue Neuve des Mathurins, you could get a first-class dinner for ten francs, a bowl of soup for two-and-a-half. There were no frills: if you wanted a tablecloth, you paid extra! By the time old Duval died, the business was worth ten million francs, all of which he had salted away outside Paris. Young Duval had spent the war years and the months of the Commune in the south of France, but now returned to find three of his Bouillons had survived un-damaged, but that the supplies to set them going again were still in very short supply. He did a deal, as I later discovered, with an Englishman and diverted into his restaurants much food intended for the starving poor, but soon found himself unable to get together sufficient meat or vegetables to satisfy them, and business was falling off – he even had, temporarily, to close two of them.

It was at this time that he first called on me, at the new, smaller house I had taken in the Rue des Bassins. He was a slim man, who looked much older than his years, with his neat little drooping moustache and an almost bald head.

Entering the room, he sat on an upright chair, placed his top hat at his feet, and folded his hands in his lap. I had dressed in the most becoming of my dresses, the only one I had been able yet to have really carefully cleaned after its being crammed into a press for some years, and was quite ready to receive an invitation to entertain him in the way I knew best.

We took a glass of wine, and I waited for him to broach the subject. To my surprise he seemed embarrassed (not a quality I have often observed in the rich), and at length muttered that he had heard that I might be, 'temporarily, of course', financially embarrassed, and that he came with a proposition which would enable me to repair my fortune and once more support myself in the manner which had once dazzled all France. He asked that I would hear him out before giving my reply to his proposition, which he was aware I might regard with disfavour. He had several contacts in the butchery and vegetable business, outside Paris, who might be prepared to supply his Bouillons, but who were in no need of money, having prospered during the war. Seeking a way in which to get their good will, he had to offer them some special inducement, and proposed, in short, that I should be the bribe!

Many would have stopped him there and then; but I must confess that his effrontery amused me, and I permitted him to continue. He proposed that he should offer his contacts an introduction to whom he was pleased to call 'the most famous woman of love in all France', on condition that he should be granted an exclusive contract with them for the goods they could supply. My part was an obvious one. He was aware that he was asking the greatest favour of me; I would not be the sufferer; he hoped that *this* would perhaps persuade me.

'This' was a square object which was carefully wrapped,

and which he laid upon a table, then rising making his bow and leaving. I was aware of him as a man of very consider-able wealth, and confess that it was with interest I opened his gift. Had he offered himself as a lover, I would instantly have complied; to become a common hireling, however, was another matter. However – his gift: I opened the parcel, to find it was simply a book, bound in leather and gold, with the title *Les Riches de la Vie*. I was not amused, and threw it into the fireplace. However, after a while, thinking that the binding at least was attractive, I picked it up, and on putting it down on the table it fell open, and I saw that its pages were banknotes – one thousand franc banknotes – and one hundred of them.

I cannot say that I found the four men M. Duval introduced charming. The most prominent of them was the butcher, very like one of the bulls in which he dealt. Invited to tea, he simply swept aside the table, threw me to the bed, and butted me there and then without removing even his coat, much less his breeches. One of the others was the owner of a vast farm from which he supplied vegetables. He was so nervous that on the first occasion he spent himself as I loosened his waistband. A third, another farmer, was so old that he contented himself with sitting in a chair frigging himself while I posed before him; and the fourth, while virile enough, was entirely without delicacy and, exciting me with his vigour, invariably left me unsatisfied.

When the time came for M. Duval to present me with another book, it turned out to contain sufficient to enable me to return to the Rue de Chaillot, but to a new house at No 101. Thinking that the time might come when he no longer needed the services of the four suppliers, I thought it polite as an insurance to command Duval's attentions, and to cut the story short, succeeded without too much difficulty in doing so, for he had not previously had much time for love, and even the simplest devices pleased as much as startled him. Now, his Bouillons once more successful, and supplies becoming (as I had thought) more easily obtained, he turned his full attention to satisfying a newly acquired lust, and though never an acceptable lover when compared to the men of a higher class and a larger experience, at least was the means of my acquiring a house at Maisons Lafitte, several carriages, a new stable of horses, and some pleasant jewels.

Lacking in finesse, he was for a time the most enthusiastic lover I had ever had, making his appointments in advance and demanding that I should ready myself for him by undressing before his arrival. Scarcely waiting to be inside the front door, he would begin to tear off his clothes as the footman was showing him upstairs, and on entering the bedroom where I waited, would throw himself on his knees before me, seizing me by the buttocks and pressing his face between my thighs. It scarcely seemed possible that this was the same man who was so cool and distant at our first meeting.

He was violently jealous, dismissing his four suppliers and insisting that I should see them no more (a condition I was happy to accede to), and also requesting me to keep away from any former admirers who might wish to return to me. This was a greater difficulty, for Paris was beginning to be gay again, the theatres re-opened, and society once more collecting itself – so that I was once more going about, and my old friends of the male sex could not understand my reluctance to greet them as enthusiastically as they wished to greet me.

At last, Duval seemed to be treating me much more like a husband than a lover. For some weeks he came to me regularly, but without a gift of any kind; I made discreet enquiries, and heard that he was in some difficulty financially, that the restaurants were in fact mortgaged, and that his friends spoke of him as 'ruined' by me – though of course he was ruined by himself, for if he could not afford to support me, he was free to announce his departure.

The last act was played in December 1872. On the morning of the 17th, the servant had come to me at midday and announced 'a gentleman' who refused to give his name. To my delight, into the room, brisk and handsome as ever, came Hurion! We lunched together, and drank a good bottle of Bordeaux, then celebrated the warmth of our friendship and our mutual happiness at our survival of our various adventures, in the way in which you might expect. To be short, Hurion proved his vigour unimpaired by his various adventures first against the Prussians, then, later, as a spy against the Commune – in which form he explained he had often longed to call upon me, but feared discovery. Afterwards he lay upon his back in a half-doze, and I was leaning over him running my fingers through the well-remembered mat of black hair upon his hard belly and chest, and considering how best to tell him of the dreadful end of his friend and mine, Brunet, when there was a scuffle outside the door, which burst open to reveal Duval, pushing his way past the footman, and advancing towards the bed. I had forgotten he was to be here!

Immediately fully awake, Hurion leaped to his feet and seized the protesting Duval by the coat, lifting him bodily into the air despite his wriggling and striking. I could not help laughing as I saw his red protesting face over Hurion's shoulder as he strode to the door, his naked back ridged with strong muscles. What chance had the effete Duval? I heard a clatter outside, clearly signifying Duval's descent of the stairs in an undignified manner, then the slamming and bolting of the front door. Hurion returned, and excited as I was by his display of strength, I welcomed him with enthusiasm, so that in a moment he was pleased to display the strength of his manhood in another way than wrestling with a male opponent! My lips could scarce encompass him; but happily, unlike most men, Hurion was impatient of that form of tribute, for the place of a plough was in the furrow (he said) and once more demonstrated that in that respect he was untiring.

That evening at six o'clock, when Hurion had left me, Duval came again to the house; I had instructed the servants neither to admit him nor his 'friends', and Hurion had promised his protection. Next day it poured with rain; but nevertheless he returned, to be turned away once more. This time he only pretended to leave, rang again, and producing a pistol forced his way in. I was in my sitting-room preparing to receive some ladies for tea. Duval stormed in, and demanded to be returned to my favour. I told him I had done his business for him; that his Bouillons had been saved as a result; and that I was scarcely to be blamed if he had not the sense to pay attention to his work.

'And for myself?' he pleaded. He was ridiculous. I reminded him that it was I who had introduced him to passion, but that I had never pretended to love him. He was at liberty to display his newly acquired skill elsewhere.

All this time he had been holding his pistol against his thigh. Privately, I suspected it to be unloaded, for he had never seemed to me a man of violence. Now he raised it, pressed it against his left side, and pulled the trigger. There was an explosion, and he fell to the ground. I ran forward and lifted him. He was still breathing, but blood was pouring from his wound on to the carpet.

Fortunately, Hurion arrived a few minutes later, and sending for Duval's servants had him carried to his own house, where a bullet was found to be lodged in his back just below his lung. I was frankly glad to be rid of him, having lost all sympathy with him.

Two days later, as I lay in bed with Hurion, who had consented for the time to stay with me night and day, a Prefect of Police visited me. Pulling the curtains around the bed, I put on a gown and received him, Hurion overhearing all that transpired. The Prefect, to my amazement, announced that I was banished from France! Foolishly, perhaps, I attempted to reach an agreement with him, but he proved unyielding, and simply laid a document confirming the sentence upon the table before leaving.

I attempted, during the next two days, to get the decision revoked. I called upon Duval (could I have abased myself more?) to ask him to intercede: he declined to see me, though at his bedside, I was told by his nurse, Mme Armann, that he kept several of my small gifts to him in his view. Descending the staircase of his house, I met his mother, who immediately violently attacked me for causing the death of her son (who, in fact was to recover perfectly, and as far as I know is still alive).[1]

Hurion was of the opinion that someone more powerful and important than M. Duval wanted, for his own reasons, to get me out of France. I was not entirely sorry to have an excuse to leave, honourably, a field of battle which had sadly changed during the past ten years. I was now thirty years old,[2] and there was a new generation of public women, less delicate in their sensibilities than we of the Second Empire had been, less willing to live and let live, and determined to raise themselves in society. It seemed that one or more of them had been spreading rumours about the whole Duval affair: perhaps even that I had shot him! – though one story also said that, on seeing him fall, I

[1] he died in 1922, described in an obituary in *The Times* as 'the last real boulevardier'.

[2] actually, thirty-five

had said to Hurion: 'The pig might have done it in the outer room and spared my carpet!' Of course Hurion had not even been present at the time of the shooting, and even though I certainly remarked to him later that the carpet had not been improved by the blood spilled upon it, it was not a great concern of mine since the carpet was in any case due to be renewed.

I closed the house, and left for London within the week, saying a farewell to Hurion, now the only man in Paris I was sorry to leave. The Prince was there, and provided me with enough money (as well as a present of some diamond buckles, which he orderd for me in the Burlington Arcade and which were to be dispatched to me in the South of France) to stay for a week at the Grosvenor Hôtel, which this time seemed pleased enough to entertain me. I then left for Nice, having received a message from Caro Letessier, presently living there in a beautiful villa taken for her by the son of the Prince of Monaco. And to her I went; and it is in her villa that I have written down these memories.

Not long after my arrival here, I heard that my house in the Rue de Chaillot had been sold and its contents auctioned, allegedly to pay my debts, which it was reported in *Figaro* amounted to above eighteen thousand francs. My pictures, silver, vases, statues, my mahogany bed, the oriental curtains which came from the Prince's room at the Exposition – all were dispersed. Yet did anyone profit honourably from the sale? – for I have no doubt the promissory notes brandished by the cutlers, drapers, dressmakers were forged.

I have made friends here. Caro, the sweetest of companions, has introduced me to society in Monaco, and a number of gentlemen – among them Englishmen of the best society, who to a great extent favour this town during the winter months – have become my friends. I may remain here; the climate is pleasant, and it is possible to live well here at a tiny proportion of the sum one must spend in Paris. Yet I long for the more febrile excitement of that city, the centre of the world. We shall see.

ENVOI

Cora Pearl never again recovered her position in society, nor was she ever again able to live so luxuriously. In 1874 she sold her house at 101, Rue de Chaillot to another friend of Caroline Letessier, Blanche d'Antigny, a carpenter's daughter who for a time became almost as successful a courtesan as Cora had been at her height. For a while, Cora survived in reasonable comfort, though in 1877 she was forced to sell her silver, and in 1880 lost the last of her wealthy protectors, and had grown ugly of face, though her body was still well preserved and supple. In 1881 the latter fact was confirmed when a young Englishman, Julian Arnold, the son of a *Daily Telegraph* leader-writer, befriended 'an old woman' he found weeping on a kerb-stone in Monte Carlo. He gave her shelter, and she in return entertained him and his friends with anecdotes about some of her lovers. It was Cora Pearl, and later that night she came to Mr Arnold's study, clad only in a borrowed man's dressing-gown which to his embarrass-ment she removed to reveal her naked body; she wished, she said, to show him that if she had lost everything else, that at least was still beautiful. (Mr Arnold was still alive in the early 'fifties, and must have been one of the last men living to have had that particular experience of one of the great Second Empire courtesans.)

Despite that rather melancholy story, Cora Pearl seems to have lived comfortably almost until her death, helped, one biographer suggested, by the support of some of her erstwhile colleagues, and perhaps by members of the Jockey Club, who are said to have subscribed for a pension. She sold the Château de Beauséjour in 1885 (by which time it was heavily mortgaged), and in the following year published the *Mémoires*, written in Paris, at 8, Rue de Bassano, where she was living in a third-floor flat. Though kindly received by most critics, the book was too tame to make her any money – though it sufficiently embarrassed her aged father, then living in Baltimore.

Cora Pearl died on 8 July, 1886, of cancer. There were obituary notices in British and French newspapers and magazines, most of them surprisingly generous. Her funeral, which cost £38, was paid for by 'some former admirers' (an English newspaper reported), and she was buried at Batignolles cemetery. Three months later, crowds gathered at the salerooms of the Hôtel Druot to bid for her *lingerie* and bed-linen, a single pearl necklace, Lansac's portrait of her on horseback, a whip and riding-habit, eighty books and several blonde wigs.

W. B.